Alec Issigonis

ANDREW NAHUM

The Design Council

Alec Issigonis

First published 1988 in the United Kingdom by
The Design Council
28 Haymarket
London SW1Y 4SU

Typeset by Colset Pte Ltd, Singapore
Printed by Jolly & Barber Ltd, Rugby

© Andrew Nahum 1988

British Library CIP Data
Nahum, Andrew
    Alec Issigonis.——(Modern European
    designers series).
    1. Issigonis, Alec   2. Automobile designers
    ——Great Britain——Biography
    I. Title   II. Design Council   III. Series
    629.2'31'0924   TL140.I/

ISBN 0 85072 172 5

Contents

Mini car – major recognition.
Alec Issigonis on the occasion when his knighthood was conferred, 27 August 1969.

Acknowledgements

The author wishes to thank Sir Alec Issigonis for constructive comments on the draft typescript, and Rodney Bull at the Rover Group for his help. Dr Alex Moulton, Jack Daniels, Ron Unsworth and Chris Kingham were generous with their recollections of working with Sir Alec, and Christopher Dowson gave kind assistance with archival and illustrative material.

The author and publishers wish to express special thanks to the BBC Hulton Picture Library, the British Motor Industry Heritage Trust (Austin Rover Group), the National Motor Museum at Beaulieu and Quadrant Picture Library for permission to reproduce illustrative material here.

Introduction

Sir Alec Issigonis is the best-known British car designer and virtually the only one with an international reputation. More importantly, from the perspective of this monograph, his work provoked a change in attitude towards automotive design. For many years, the industrial design profession regarded car work merely as meretricious styling – the application of superficial decoration. This was due partly to the diffusion into Europe of American inventions like 'planned obsolescence', the yearly model change and the jet-plane styling devised at General Motors. But both the Morris Minor and the Mini were 'honest' cars offering genuine improvements in utility, and the Mini maximised interior room to an extent that had never before been achieved in such a small car.

Issigonis always professed that functionalism was his only goal, and the results proved to the wider design profession that car design was a purposeful and valid activity. He accumulated numerous honours, being elected a Royal Designer to Industry in 1964, and is also a Fellow of the Royal Society, for 'Services to Science and its Application'. In 1969 he was knighted. He seems to view these honours with a quirky sense of irony: 'Cars are so boring' he once remarked, and on the occasion of his 80th birthday, when asked whether he regarded himself as an engineer, a scientist or an architect, he replied 'an ironmonger'.

His approach to design is not theory-laden, but of a piece with his belief in the common sense and abilities of the practical engineer. Issigonis was perhaps the last major motor industry designer to be able to originate new cars in an idiosyncratic and personal way. He never believed that a designer should work in response to market researchers, product planning committees and academic ergonomists, and was lucky to be able to develop his projects with small teams, which he controlled directly. He asserts: 'A designer has only to make a good car that satisfies him, and if he is a practical man it will satisfy the world.'[1]

Chronology

1906	Born in Smyrna, Turkey, of a Greek father and a German mother. His father ran a marine engineering business, and was himself an engineer and designer.
1912	Sees a Blériot 11 flying.
1920 (circa)	First drive in a motor car (a Cadillac).
1922	Turkish nationalists force the flight of foreign residents. The Issigonis family are evacuated to Malta as refugees.
1923	Issigonis arrives in London. Enrols at Battersea Polytechnic to study engineering.
1928	Takes first job in the motor industry as draughtsman with Edward Gillett, London, inventor of an 'easy change' gearbox.
1934–36	Draughtsman at Rootes Motors. Begins experimental design work on independent front suspension for cars. Begins construction, with friend George Dowson, of his own competition car, the Lightweight Special.
1936	Joins Morris Motors as suspension designer.
1943	Hand-built prototype of the Minor (initially called the Mosquito) constructed at Cowley.
1948	Morris Minor launched. It is considered a huge advance in space, roadholding and 'driveability' over conventional small cars.
1950 (circa)	Issigonis instigates the construction of an experimental front-wheel drive Morris Minor. Becomes Chief Engineer, Morris Motors.
1952	Moves to Alvis. Designs new luxury eight-cylinder car. It does not reach production.
1955	Asked by Leonard Lord to become Chief Engineer of BMC (formed by the merger of Austin and Morris).
1957	Starts design of 'a proper miniature car'. This is intended to compete with the 'bubble cars' that enjoyed a sales boom following the Suez crisis.
1959	Mini launched, after two-year 'crash' programme.
1962	Morris 1100 launched, using Issigonis layout, and involvement of Pininfarina for bodywork. It is to become Britain's best-selling car.
1964	Elected a Royal Designer for Industry. Awarded the CBE.
1964–69	Becomes Engineering Director of BMC. Austin 1800, 3 litre and Maxi launched.
1968	Leyland Motors, under Donald Stokes, takes over BMC.
1969–71	Works on 'steam Mini' and various engine projects.
1971	Retires, but continues to work as consultant to the company, with a small development team. Makes comments on all new models developed, and plans improvements to the Mini. Develops a 'gearless Mini'.

Issigonis with the Lightweight Special. The venue is the paddock at Shelsley Walsh, June 1946. The car in front is a Lancia Aprilia.

GUY GRIFFITHS

Early Life and a Start in the Motor Industry

'Issigonis is an extremely cultivated man, wide-ranging in his conversation, perceptive in his judgements, gently mocking in his wit. . . . Of his intelligence and intellect, there can be no doubt whatever. One sometimes wonders what a gentle man like this is doing in the motor industry.'[2] In fact, many turns of fate brought him from Smyrna (today's Izmir) in Turkey to the English Midlands, where he designed some of Britain's most popular and influential cars.

Alec Issigonis was born in Smyrna in 1906. His father, Constantine, was Greek, one of the great number then in Western Turkey. However, he had become naturalised as a Briton when living and studying in England as a young man, reputedly because he enjoyed life in England so much, only returning to the family business on the death of his father in 1922. His mother, Hulda, was a powerful and impressive woman, the daughter of a Bavarian family that had built the brewery in Smyrna.

Growing up in the Ottoman Empire in the early years of this century did not mean that the young Issigonis was cut off from mechanical influences. His father and uncle had a marine engineering business in Smyrna, where they made, among other things, engines and pumps for ships. In 1912, aged six, he was taken to see a

ISSIGONIS/COURTESY MRS GEORGE DOWSON

Romantic fantasy. A study for a front-engined racing car, done in the mid-1930s. The original is in pencil and colour wash.

great wonder – the famous French display pilot Adolphe Pegoud, demonstrating his Blériot 11 from a nearby racecourse. The young boy became fascinated by engineering. 'My father always had a drawing-board in his dressing-room', he recalled, 'As a little boy I used to go and watch him drawing, and when I was quite, quite small I was determined to become an engineer.'[3]

When Turkey entered the First World War on the German side the British community was interned. This included the Issigonis family, and their property was expropriated.

After the war things began to return to normal, and in this period young Issigonis saw his first motor car – a Cadillac belonging to the Chairman of Standard Oil in Smyrna. 'They had a Greek chauffeur and he was my fan . . . he used to take me for rides in it. . . . I was absolutely enthralled by this car.'[4]

The post-war peace conference at Versailles in 1919 awarded a coastal strip of Anatolia to Greece, but this did not help the fortunes of the Greek population. Enraged by this affront to national pride, Atatürk and his followers drove the Greek Army out, and in 1922 the Issigonis family and the rest of the British community were evacuated by the Royal Navy to Malta.

Alec Issigonis was then brought by his mother to London. Though encouraged to go to art school by friends who were impressed by his obvious skill at drawing, he insisted on studying engineering, and enrolled at Battersea Polytechnic in 1923. His father, meanwhile, was ill in Malta, and died on Hulda's return. She then travelled back to Smyrna to see what could be rescued from the business, sold the land and returned to London. She was to keep house for Alec for many years and to be a powerful influence on his life.

At Battersea Issigonis failed to obtain a degree, and scraped through a diploma course instead. This was a legacy of his erratic schooling, for as an internee and refugee he had received virtually no formal education. His greatest stumbling-block was mathematics. 'All creative people hate mathematics' and 'mathematicians are not creative people' are remarks he has often repeated. Later in life he took great pride in being able to succeed at design without 'being hampered' by academic expertise.

Issigonis began to attend lectures and meetings at the Institution of Automotive Engineers and, through its Secretary, was put in touch with Edward Gillett, an inventor who was developing a semi-automatic type of gearbox. Thus in 1928 Issigonis started his first job in the motor industry. He not only worked at a drawing-board in Gillett's office in Victoria Street, London, but also toured the motor industry attempting to sell the device. At the time, when most cars were fitted with 'crash' boxes which took some skill to master, there was much interest in 'easy change' systems and the Humber company began to study the Gillett device. However, the development of synchromesh by General Motors sounded the death knell for Gillett's system (and many others). This work brought Issigonis into contact with the mainstream industry, and in particular with the Humber Chief Designer T Wishart, who in 1934 persuaded him to join their design department.

At Humber much attention was being given to an American innovation – independent front suspension (IFS) introduced into Britain by Maurice Olley, an ex-Rolls-Royce engineer who had moved to General Motors. Though most British manufacturers were wedded to the rigid 'beam axle', the Rootes brothers who controlled Humber had come into the manufacturing business as successful motor dealers. They understood the sales appeal of a superior suspension system, and encouraged the design department to develop one. Issigonis was particularly interested in suspension problems, so Wishart assigned him to the job, where he worked under Bill Heynes, who was later to be head engineer at Jaguar. Issigonis stayed for two years with Humber, building an experimental Hillman Minx with independent front suspension. He also became acquainted with Maurice Olley, who had been moved by General Motors to Luton. Olley helped Issigonis develop his thinking on independent front suspension. Issigonis's ideas were incorporated into Humber's 1936 'Even Keel' models, which were among the first mass-produced British cars with independent front suspension.

However, while Issigonis was becoming familiar with suspension design at Humber, he also embarked on a project in his leisure hours that was to give him a much greater personal understanding of suspension behaviour – the design and construction of his own racing and hillclimb car – the Lightweight Special.

COURTESY MRS GEORGE DOWSON

'I was really weaned on Austin Sevens.' Issigonis competing in a speed hillclimb with his 'Ulster' sports model, sometime in the early 1930s. The venue is probably Shelsley Walsh.

From the same era as the Lightweight Special, sketches for an unbuilt rear-engined racing car which seems to owe something to Auto-Union influence. Side pods form large ducts for cooling air gathered at the scoops in the nose.

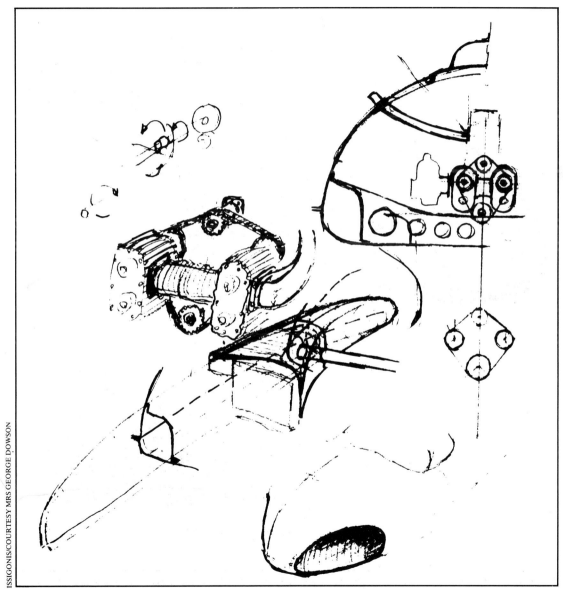

Sketches exploring two-stage supercharging for the rear-engined car, and a method for driving the two Roots blowers by chain.

COURTESY MRS GEORGE DOWSON

Issigonis entertaining his friend George Dowson's daughter, Penny, with a model aeroplane he had made. Taken sometime in the 1950s.

Issigonis (right) with friends at the Trout Inn, Godstow, near Oxford, c.1955.

Issigonis (right) with his mother, Hulda (centre) and friends, outside their flat in Five Mile Drive, Oxford in the mid-1950s.

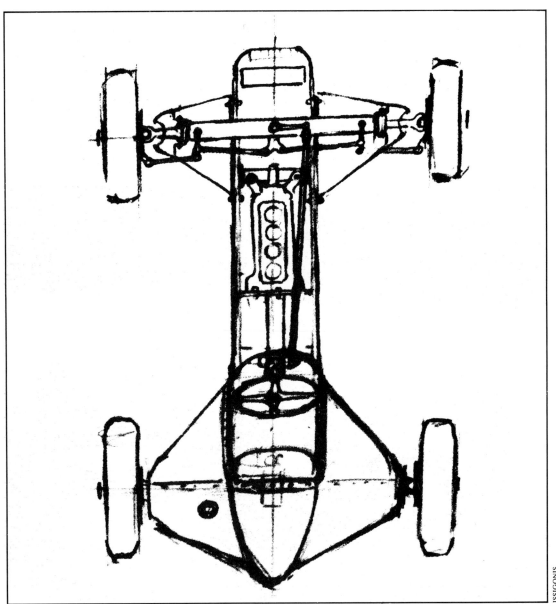

The Lightweight Special. Plan view.

The Lightweight Special

From about 1930 Issigonis had started to race a supercharged 'Ulster' model Austin Seven sports car, which he gradually developed, eventually fitting his own pattern of independent front suspension. With his friend George Dowson, who worked at English Electric, he then decided to build a competition car from scratch, to his own design, and incorporating independent suspension both front and rear. (At the time, many factory-built racing cars did not use independent suspension, though some experimental conversions were tried.) The result of Dowson's and Issigonis's labour was the Lightweight Special. The celebrated motoring writer John Bolster described it as 'perhaps . . . the most amazing special ever built. It has the appearance of having been built regardless of cost, in the racing department of some great factory, whereas it is the result of sheer hard labour in a little shed, with no proper equipment whatsoever.'[5] Initially the work was done in the garage of the house Issigonis shared with his

Issigonis winning one of the first races held in Britain after the Second World War at Gransden Lodge, 1946.

mother in Kenilworth. However, during construction Issigonis took a new job, at Morris Motors, and the car had to be moved to the new home in Abingdon. The project was started in 1933 and took until 1938, since the pair had no power tools and did everything themselves, but once on the track the car immediately began to win its class.

Hillclimbing, in the inter-war years, was a popular form of motor sport. Many major manufacturers entered, but numerous amateurs also built cars. Particular interest was added to the sport both by the technical ingenuity exercised by the constructors, and the fact that these 'specials' were often able to defeat the might of racing departments of major manufacturers. Through Murray Jamieson, designer of the famous supercharged Austin Seven racing engines, Dowson and Issigonis were able to

obtain one of the 'blown' works side-valve engines. The success of the chassis design was displayed when, a few months before the war, the Lightweight beat the Austin factory entry at Prescott, using an identical power unit.

Issigonis had saved weight on the car by devising a very efficient 'stressed skin' structure, which dispensed with the massive but flexible 'ladder' chassis which was then a standard feature. This scheme was extremely original, at a time when even high performance racing cars used a ladder chassis. The compliance of the chassis contributed to the suspension and ride of these cars, though its behaviour could not easily be predicted at the design stage. However, with very firm road springs and inspired tuning, this traditional scheme could give fine road holding. Issigonis, though, knew from his suspension work that the best system would be to make the

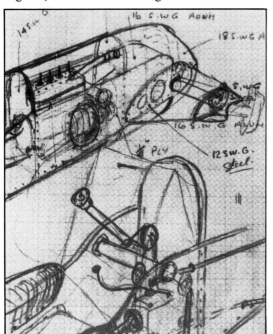

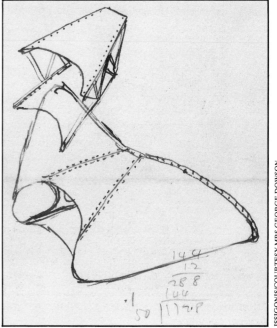

chassis as rigid as possible, and to design the suspension system to provide all the compliance. This represented a move away from empirical chassis and suspension design. (In the 'big league', Auto Union and Mercedes Benz were, of course, also doing this with their famous Grand Prix cars of the period.)

The body sides of the Lightweight were of plywood, covered on the outside with aluminium sheeting – a technique perhaps borrowed from contemporary aircraft construction. Issigonis also displayed his ingenuity by making virtually every other component also carry some of the structural load. Thus the seat pan tied the body sides together, as did the engine and the rear axle (differential) casing. For the suspension, Issigonis devised a highly original, fully independent system using rubber as a springing medium. At the rear, swing axles were restrained by rubber loops in tension. At the front, double wishbones worked bell-cranks which compressed rubber discs located within a tubular cross-member.

The use of rubber was highly unconventional, but remarkably prophetic. Decades later, the revolutionary Mini was to be suspended on Moulton rubber units. For the hillclimb car, the rubber springs had the advantage of ultra-light weight, compared with steel 'cart' or coil springs, as well as a rising spring rate. This means that the deflection is not proportional to load, but that the rubber stiffens as load increases – a desirable characteristic for a competition car. Rubber also has the useful property of a degree of self-damping.

Unfortunately, the outbreak of war cut short the Lightweight's career just as the car and drivers Issigonis and Dowson were getting into

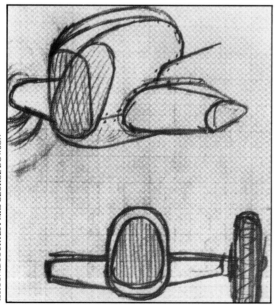
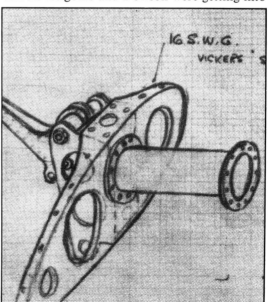

ISSIGONIS/COURTESY MRS GEORGE DOWSON

Lightweight Special. Assembly sketches for sheet metal components and (above) *for the nearside front suspension.*

their stride, and all motor sport stopped 'for the duration'. (Issigonis's war-time activities are covered in the next chapter.) After hostilities ceased Issigonis came first in one of the earliest post-war races, at Gransden Lodge in 1946, and several successful hillclimb seasons followed when the car usually won the 750 cc class, and often the 1100 cc class as well. Eventually, as chief engineer of Morris Motors in 1948, Issigonis succumbed to company pressure to desist from competition, on account of 'increased duties'.

Through the Lightweight project, Issigonis

made, in the Dowson family, some of his closest friends. There he was very different to the autocratic designer 'with an arrogant belief in doing things his way' that he became in the motor industry. They describe him as 'a charming man with a wonderful sense of humour – quite unique.'[6] He became godfather to George's daughter (and took her to the launch of the Mini – a great treat!). Most weekends he would travel to Worcestershire to stay at the Dowsons' farm, often bringing experimental cars. (The prototype Mini often came down, in camouflage.) The family and Issigonis would also travel to-

COURTESY MRS GEORGE DOWSON

'The appearance of having been built, regardless of cost, in the racing department of some great factory.' This view shows how the body sides form the main structural members. Rear axle (differential), seat pan, and dash all tie the sides together and give rigidity.

gether – several times to Monte Carlo and also skiing: 'he was fun, great fun.'

Much later Issigonis described the Light-weight as 'a frivolity in my life. It was not so much a design exercise as a means of teaching me to use my hands. George and I learned the hard way how to build something for ourselves from scratch.'

Nevertheless, the importance of the project to the development of Issigonis as a designer was probably greater than he admits. Performance and roadholding were not high priorities in the industry at the time, and competition gave Issigonis direct experience of designing for these criteria. Both the Morris Minor and the Mini were to be distinguished by roadholding and 'driveability' which were greatly superior to other contemporary products. Competition gave Issigonis the experience to become an informed judge of road behaviour and handling. The project must also have contributed to his understanding of the development of efficient 'box' structures – a talent he was to display years later with the body engineering of the Mini.

COURTESY MRS GEORGE DOWSON

The offside front suspension. Compare this photograph with the drawing on page 15.

Issigonis and the Lightweight Special at an early post-war hillclimb meeting.

KLEMANTASKI

The celebrated Morris Minor began as a war-time project by Issigonis for a popular car, and was originally known as the Mosquito. This production Minor was built in 1946.

Morris and the Minor

In 1936 Issigonis was approached with the offer of a job at Morris Motors. Robert Boyle, the chief engineer, had been sent to Detroit to study engineering methods, and returned advocating a greater division of labour at the design stage. As Issigonis recalls, Boyle returned from his study visit 'and told Lord [Managing Director] this was the way to do it, so it was decided to start separate departments for engine, gearbox, suspension, chassis – and the back axle, of all things. He fixed up other people to run the first four, and finally was left with me and the back axle. I said: "Not on your bloody life, . . . but I'll do the suspension if you like." So the wretched suspension man was switched over to back axles and I was given the suspension.'

In later life Issigonis had little time for this American system: 'They do everything the wrong way, yet do it well in the end by trampling their problems to death. Everything is sectionalised: engine, gearbox, suspension, chassis, body . . . there is nobody on top to put it all together – except the stylists.'[7] He preferred the 'one-man' car, built according to a single designer's conception (his own!), working with a small and faithful team. In fact Issigonis was himself to design several complete cars, including power units, but the economics of tooling and production were never to allow him to bring them into existence without accepting 'off the shelf' engines from the company's existing inventory.

At Morris, Issigonis's experience in vehicle suspension now started to bear fruit. Though it was a rarity among British volume car manufacturers, fully independent suspension was gaining ground in competition (Issigonis had used it on his own Lightweight Special) and independent front suspension was becoming increasingly common on American cars and on the Continent. Issigonis started experiments to develop independent front suspension for Morris production cars.

With a traditional beam axle, if one wheel passes over a bump, the wheel at the other end of the axle will suffer some disturbance. This can reduce its grip, or create false steering effects that the driver has not invited. It was clear that if each wheel could respond to the road surface without disturbing its pair, both roadholding and comfort would improve. Obviously fully independent suspension would be the ideal, but initially, achieving independent suspension of the front wheels was seen to be the objective, for it promised to bring the greatest benefits to cornering ability and the fidelity of the steering.

Undoubtedly independent suspension was the coming thing, and at Morris Issigonis was joined by the MG designer H N Charles, who had conceived the R-type MG racing car of 1934. This had independent suspension by torsion bars, and though advanced in conception and full of potential, the car was axed when MG pulled out of racing. (Issigonis, in fact, did not consider it to be very good.) However, from the R-type project came Jack Daniels. He became Issigonis's right-hand man, and was of enormous importance in the execution of his car designs. So, fortuitously, Morris Motors had acquired a team with advanced ideas on suspension. Daniels personally interpreted a large proportion of the famous Issigonis sketches, converting them into dimensioned working drawings, and became, in effect, manager of the development projects. Issigonis called him 'the best all-round draughtsman in the country',[8] and Alex Moulton observed 'One man can achieve exactly zero without an effective team who are inspired to be pointing in the same direction.'[9] Daniels's contribution ranged from the interpretation of Issigonis's initial ideas down to the detailed development of every part. Daniels just says 'His was the inspiration, and mine was the perspiration.'[10]

Surprisingly, not all early IFS systems worked as well as good beam axle suspensions. The beam axle had considerable virtues – it ensured particularly that both wheels of a pair always pointed in the same direction. In effect, the length (equal to the track of the car) and strength of the axle beam made it relatively easy to control unwanted deflections of the wheels induced by cornering, braking forces and road shocks. However, this was only true with stiff 'vintage' type leaf springs. The trend towards softer sprung cars in the 1930s showed up weaknesses. Soft springs resulted in poorer axle location, leading to inferior road-holding caused by 'false' steering effects from bumps and body roll.

The answer was an independent suspension system to locate the wheels accurately, using wishbones and a rigid body shell to provide a firm base for the suspension to work from. However, it took some time to evolve the correct geometry and stiffness for these items to make the new system significantly better than the 'vintage' arrangement.

It was also found helpful for directional stability, as demonstrated by Olley, to bias the weight of the car to the front wheels, unlike traditional cars where the engine was set well back in the chassis. This would lead to a reduction in traction from the rear wheels, though it was to prove an asset with front-wheel drive – a system that Issigonis was soon to investigate.

Issigonis has said of his work at this time:

'When I was middle-aged [ie thirty!], I was doing research work at Morris and had a pretty free hand on the development of suspension and chassis problems in general. At that time I had converted some experimental cars to independent front-wheel suspension, and . . . came across the deadly hazard of directional instability. Very little was known about this problem in those days but by continual effort and experimentation, I eventually got a bad-handling car to steer to my satisfaction by making it nose-heavy. Modern experimenters will be horrified at such a crude approach, but to me the effect was so dramatic that I never forgot it.'[11]

For the 1938 Morris Ten Issigonis worked on an independent coil spring suspension, but in the event a cheaper beam axle was selected for production. It seems that the company had bought a Chrysler for evaluation at the time, which rode exceptionally well on beam axles. The behaviour of this car persuaded the financial management to over-ride the opinions of its engineers and insist on the simpler beam axle arrangement for Morris cars. Issigonis was not to see his ideas on independent suspension used in production at Morris until after the war, when this design was fitted to the small MG Y-type saloon and subsequently was adapted for the MGB.

With the outbreak of war, Morris became heavily involved in military work. (It became The Nuffield Organization in 1940.) As a member of a reserved occupation Issigonis stayed at Cowley, and with his small experimental unit was put to work on a variety of military projects, including a motorised wheelbarrow for air-dropping to paratroops, intended to allow them to take 500 lb loads along jungle tracks. There was also an amphibious version in which he was towed out to sea by no-nonsense Navy men to test the claims made for it. At the time there was something of a fashion among amateur strategists for dreaming up unlikely war-winning mechanical inventions, and nothing came of this one. Issigonis was also

NATIONAL MOTOR MUSEUM

The 1937 Morris 10. A staple of Morris production during Issigonis's early years with the company. He proposed an independent front suspension design for the car, but this feature was not adopted on any Morris car until after the war.

THE AUSTIN ROVER GROUP (B.M.I.H.T.)

Issigonis in 1944, testing the amphibious motorised wheelbarrow developed for the armed forces.

'The best all-round draughtsman in the country', according to Issigonis. Jack Daniels, chief draughtsman on both the Minor and Mini projects, and right-hand man to Issigonis, photographed in 1986 with the preliminary scale model of the car. Unusually, the model is made of sheet brass – the only occasion on which Daniels can remember this being used. Top Right: An early sketch (c.1942) by Issigonis for the Mosquito. It shows the original narrow track and bulbous wings which were slimmed down by the time the first models were built.

largely responsible for the design of the Morris lightweight reconnaissance vehicle (a kind of Jeep) that was under development for the Ministry of Defence.

In spite of the requirements of war production, the company clearly did not intend to fall behind in the production of a new popular car, for in 1942, at a time when British industry was supposed to be totally dedicated to war work, the first scale model of what was to become Issigonis's Minor was built, and drawing work must have started some time before that. In early 1943 the assembly of a hand-formed steel prototype started in the Cowley experimental body shop. The name 'Mosquito' was chosen, no doubt because of associations with the famous De Havilland fighter-bomber. (Miles Thomas, then Managing Director of Morris Motors, was very 'air-minded', having been a Royal Flying Corps pilot in the First World War. He went on subsequently to run BOAC. Issigonis thinks he chose the name.)

A more fluid system of organisation came about in many British industries under the pressure of war-time experimentation, and perhaps for that reason Issigonis had an unprecedented degree of control over the development of the new model. In his autobiography *Out on a Wing*, Miles Thomas recalled

'Working under the Chief Engineer AV Oak was a shy, reserved young man named Alec Issigonis. In spare moments . . . the three of us would sit and exchange ideas. Alec always used to put his suggestions forward in a most tentative way. He had some very fundamental new ideas about motor car construction, and the first thing we decided in the make-up of this small saloon was that we would throw away the conventional chassis, make the body take the reaction stresses from the

axles, and employ independent suspension at the front and, if possible, at the rear. . . . Clearly it would have to be unconventional.'[12]

At about this time, Issigonis designed an unusual opposed piston two-stroke engine with which he experimented, and also, for the new car, a four-stroke unit which it was hoped would give good power output, but attract low taxation. (Road tax on cars in Britain at the time was scaled according to horsepower, as calculated by a formula – the 'RAC Rating'. It was one of the vagaries of fiscal policy that this penalized cylinder bore size, rather than outright engine capacity, leading to distorted 'long stroke' engines designed to reduce tax liability.) Issigonis's engine for the Mosquito was a horizontally opposed, flat four-cylinder engine, and it was proposed to design two cylinder sizes to fit the same crankcase, giving an 1100 cc version for export and 800 cc for the UK in order to keep the horsepower tax low.

The unconventional engine was developed in the experimental unit by Issigonis and Daniels, by-passing Morris Engines Branch. Not surprisingly, the Engines Branch was not enthusiastic about this cuckoo when asked to build it. A major advantage of the flat four is smoothness, deriving from good mechanical balance, but this one seems to have suffered from poor power output and flimsy crankshaft support.

These two new engines preoccupied Issigonis for a long time. Miles Thomas recalled

'When the prototype engine was on the test bench it gave off more fumes than the factory chimney – which led to an interesting episode one bright summer's day when I wanted the opinion of Alex Issigonis, who was a particular expert on suspension systems, on the springing of a prototype

RAF reconnaissance armoured vehicle. I found him in the hush-hush test-house poring paternally over his reluctant two-stroke. I asked him if he would come out with us on the armoured vehicle. It was hay-making time. . . . Alex suffered from severe hay fever, and as soon as we came anywhere near those sweet-scented pollen-laden fields he began to feel positively miserable. He dripped everywhere: nose, eyes, and he sneezed continuously. He was a wretched sight. All the same, he rapidly put his finger on the shortcomings of the springing. . . . Back we went to the works. . . . Alex soon had his face over his fuming engine. Immediately he regained

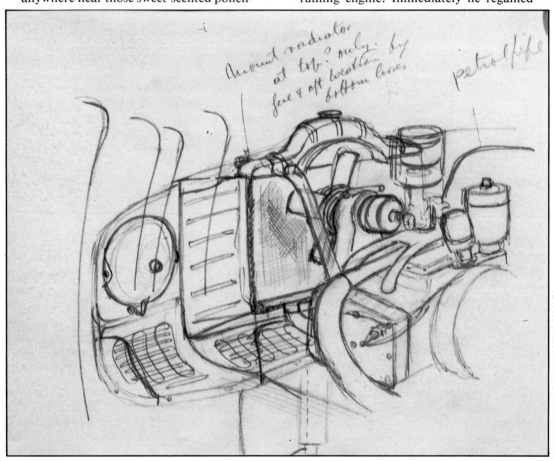

Installation sketch for Issigonis's flat four-cylinder engine in the Mosquito. Although it was not adopted for production, a legacy was an unusually wide engine bay space and excellent accessibility.

his normal composure: the oil fumes over-came his hay fever at once.'[13]

The specification that evolved for the Mosquito was entirely Issigonis's – an almost unique occurrence in the volume side of the motor industry, and Thomas deserves full credit for allowing him to pursue the project. Oak was also sympathetic, and allowed his junior complete freedom to develop the car. 'We were great friends . . . he never interfered in the slightest way',[14] said Issigonis. However, he may have been a more subtle superior than Issigonis realised. 'In my opinion,' says Jack Daniels, 'Vic Oak was very clever. He managed "Issi". He kept him on the rails. The courage to proceed came largely from him.'[15] The Minor was also

THE AUSTIN ROVER GROUP (B.M.I.H.)

Morris Motors, though ostensibly fully committed to war production, found the resources and labour to build models and a full-size running prototype of the car. Lord Nuffield 'was furious when he saw it', and called it 'the poached egg'. This static model of 1945 is close to the eventual production form.

special in being drawn up freshly as one single integrated project, without the designer having to cobble up existing chassis or suspension components in the time-honoured way of the British motor industry. 'Issi basically wanted to design everything. There was no intentional delegation, though sometimes we had to fill in', says Daniels. 'He knew what he was after, and he got it, even if it was wrong.'[16] The Mosquito was completely new, and this was exactly how Issigonis liked to work. A similarly open brief was later to give him another success with the Mini. This autocratic approach to design led to him being referred to, on occasion, as 'Arrogonis' – a sobriquet which appears to have bothered him not at all! 'Oh yes – I'm Arrogonis!'[17]

The Minor changed little between the very first sketches Issigonis made and production. In order to attain maximum stiffness for minimum weight, the body was constructed from pressed steel throughout, and had independent front suspension, sprung by torsion bars. Torsion bars were used because the long-term durability of welded-up pressed steel bodies under repeated suspension loads was not known. Coil springs would have produced higher localised stresses at the front corners of the body, whereas the torsion bars ran backwards and fed the loads into the strongest area – the centre of the chassis box. The car also embodied Issigonis's ideas on nose-heavy weight distribution and softer front springing. However, the independent rear suspension of the prototype, using swing axles and torsion bars, was abandoned on the grounds of cost. This was a probably a good thing, for unless suspension movement is severely curtailed by very hard springing, swing axles impose unwelcome camber changes on the rear wheels under acceleration and braking, which results in extremely treacherous behaviour in cornering. With a solid leaf sprung rear axle, cornering

behaviour was predictable and road-holding excellent, offering new standards of handling in a popular car, surpassing many expensive and sporting cars. This was also helped by the accurate rack and pinion steering which Issigonis adopted from the outset, to replace the then conventional steering box. The handling standards of the Minor were set by Issigonis who, according to Daniels, was 'a most exciting driver at times', and derive in part from his own involvement in competition car design. Issigonis's cars may have been designed with habitability in mind, but all show honest and accurate handling: they support the contention that it is necessary to like cars in order to engineer good ones.

As the car neared production, the name Mosquito was dropped. The smallest Morris had traditionally been called the Minor, so that became the name for Issigonis's new car. Another change was made to the power unit. Issigonis wanted the four-stroke flat four-cylinder engine he had developed for the car,

The Mosquito on test in 1946. It still has the original narrow bodyshell and track.

THE AUSTIN ROVER GROUP (B.M.I.H.T.)

and some prototypes had been built. As stated, Morris Engines did not really want to build this alien design, and it was doubtful whether the company had funds to develop and tool up for it. Finally, Miles Thomas persuaded Hugh Dalton, Chancellor of the Exchequer, that the horsepower tax (based on bore size) was biasing engine design towards inefficient long-stroke types.[18] When the tax was subsequently reformed, there was less reason to persevere with an 800 cc engine, and the car was adapted to take the existing Morris 918 cc in-line side-valve four-cylinder unit. However, a legacy of the flat four was a very wide engine bay, allowing an unusually generous amount of space and excellent accessibility.

With the Minor, Issigonis began another trend he was to continue with the Mini – the reduction of wheel size. Before the war, 17 (42 cm) and 18 inch (45 cm) rims were common on small cars. For the Minor, Issigonis asked Dunlop to produce tyres and wheels with 14 inch (35 cm) rims. There are several functional advantages in reducing wheel size: unsprung weight goes down relative to the weight of the car, and thus the suspension is better able to con-

NATIONAL MOTOR MUSEUM

The success of the original bodyshell design shows in the way that it allowed some restyling. The much-loved Morris 1000, introduced in 1956, had higher wing-mounted headlights (originally to satisfy American regulations) and a one-piece windscreen. It remained in production until 1971.

trol the movements of the wheels, leading to better ride; the roadholding also benefits from better suspension performance and from the lowered centre of gravity. Another important effect, in a small car, is the reduced intrusion of the wheel arches into the passenger cabin giving improved habitability. However, it is recorded that the main consideration with Issigonis was aesthetic – he sought to have wheels that were in proportion with the scale of the car.[19]

This aesthetic preference bears on Issigonis's oft-quoted assertion that he is 'an engineer, not a stylist'. But to most eyes, the Minor seems quite clearly 'styled', and styled in a fashion that derives, quite openly, from American cars of the 1940s such as the Chevrolet. The 'jelly mould' lines that these show spring from two influences: first, the modest diffusion of aerodynamic ideas into American volume production ('The stream-lined form is essentially ugly. . . . I don't think you can ever get the public to like it', said one Detroit engineer in the 1930s); the second was

The lines of the Minor clearly derive from a contemporary American idiom, as seen in this 1948 Chevrolet. However, the success of the Minor was in reconciling these styling elements in a far smaller car.

the adoption of unitary pressed steel bodies, based on Budd patents. (In the USA, the Budd company pioneered the use of steel pressings assembled by welding, in place of panel-beaten coachwork, assembled on a wooden underframe. The Budd system spread rapidly through the American automobile industry; in Europe, Citroën were among the first to employ it.)

When hand-beaten by artisanal methods, panels with complex double curvature were expensive and awkward to produce, and were only usually attempted for upmarket avant-garde cars, such as Jean Bugatti's Atalante models. Most pre-war coachbuilt saloons tended to maintain a certain severity of line. However,

tooling up for large-scale production of pressed steel bodies allowed more flexibility in the choice of form for a cheap car. Shallow dished panels were easy to press and withdraw from the dies, while introducing curvature gave the panels rigidity, and allowed the designer to hint at modernity. Under these influences, the outline of the American popular car softened in the 1930s and 1940s, until Virgil Exner and Harley Earl drew on jet plane symbolism in the post-war era to give their products added excitement.

This American origin of the idiom adopted by Issigonis does not in any way reduce his achievement. In fact, the Minor is not simply a scaled-down Chevrolet or Oldsmobile, for to build a

Before pressed-steel assembly techniques softened the form of popular cars, complex curves were hand formed and found only on cars for the few. (Bugatti Atlantic coupé, 1935.)

habitable small car the proportions have to be changed. In the Minor, the passenger cabin takes up a greater proportion of the total length, while the bonnet and boot have shrunk. Issigonis's success is that the Minor has a visual harmony that is rare for a small utility car of the period. Even today it looks poised and sensible, and, viewed against some of its contemporaries, seems the acme of restraint and taste.

The control Issigonis had over the appearance of the Minor, and his own aesthetic approach, is

'I designed the whole car myself – even the little knob that opens the glove box.' Note also the reeded motif on the dash – a rather endearing ornamental touch from a man who claimed 'I am an engineer, not a stylist!'

underlined by his own remarks: 'I designed the whole car myself – even the little knob that opens the glove box, and the door handles.'[20] The reference to the glove box is interesting, for the dash area is not merely a severe engineering solution. There is a strong decorative element, including a central reeded panel, and a similar motif is used to embellish the speedometer and clock mountings.

If any further evidence is necessary to support the contention that Issigonis designed to satisfy aesthetic precepts, as well as to meet functional engineering constraints, it is provided by the well-known incident in which the final width of the Minor was determined. By 1947 the car was ready for production, but Issigonis was having misgivings about the shape. 'One night, in despair, I got my mechanics to cut one right down the middle; they moved the two halves apart, and I stood some distance away saying: "No, that's too much, a little closer, closer – stop!" And the difference turned out to be four inches.'[21] It was a drastic alteration to make so late in the programme and required expensive modifications to the press tooling, which had already been made, but was incorporated into the production cars. It has been suggested that the changes were possible because a breathing space occurred in the change from the flat four to the Morris engine, though it is more likely that Lord Nuffield's equivocation about whether to put the unusually shaped car into production allowed extra time. Issigonis emphasises that it was done purely 'to get the proportions right'. He was in fact entirely correct, and it is most unlikely that the Morris Minor would have had so long a production run had it been saddled with the antique narrow track of the Morris Eight.

Perhaps we should take Issigonis's statements about styling with a pinch of salt, and understand him to mean that he is not *merely* a stylist.

THE AUSTIN ROVER GROUP (B.M.I.H.T.)

All his cars have made strong visual statements, and it would be naïve to believe that this has always been purely a by-product of seeking functionalism in engineering design. Great attention has always been paid to the final appearance and the unusual element in the design of Issigonis cars is the integration of both the engineering design and the aesthetic solution from within the same mind.

However, the appearance of the Minor was too radical for Lord Nuffield, who reportedly hated the car, and would not utter the name Issigonis, referring only to 'that foreign chap'. Issigonis recalled: 'Nuffield hated the Morris Minor as soon as he saw it, and so did all the sales people. It was humble pie when we made a million of them! He had the decency to speak to me – once. He described it as "the poached egg"! He was furious when he saw it.'[22]

Fortunately, Reginald Hanks, who replaced Miles Thomas as vice-chairman at Morris, was also enthusiastic about the new car. The reservations were eventually overcome, and the Minor was launched in October 1948. It was an immediate success (though there were all too few for sale) and created great technical interest at a time when a small car was expected to be the lowest common denominator of production engineering, devoid of any original or advanced features. As Paul Skilleter put it in *Morris Minor* (1981),

'It taught the British car-buyer . . . that power, size and sheer speed were not pre-requisites for rapid journeys. For while the acceleration of the Minor was little better than any typical pre-war family saloon, its roadholding qualities and controllability were streets ahead of virtually any other production car. . . . Over twisty by-roads . . . it was capable of keeping up with cars having perhaps three times its engine size.'[23]

Among contemporary comments, that of *The Autocar* expressed the general impression that 'the design has raised the breed of small cars to a much higher level'. *Motor* called it 'one of the fastest slow cars in existence'. Road testers enthused over the handling, economy and lack of fatigue in driving the Minor.

Over 1.6 million Minors (including vans) were eventually built before production stopped in 1971. There were various modifications during the production run, though Issigonis had little to do with this evolution. He has said 'When I have designed [a car] that pleases me . . . then I'm terribly happy; but when my studies are finished, and prototypes have been built and tested and everything seems all right – then I get slightly bored.'[24]

In 1952 the Minor acquired the 803 cc overhead valve Austin 'A'-series engine, and in 1956 there was some alteration to the body (including a single curved windscreen to replace the original split type), a redesigned interior and an enlarged engine. The car came of age with the more powerful engine, and, christened the Morris 1000, continued in this form with few changes until the end of production. The Minor floorpan and suspension were also used to produce the 1956 Wolseley 1.5 litre car, and it is a tribute to Issigonis's original design that the roadholding was still commended, although it was having to cope with considerably more power than had originally been anticipated. (The handling, however, did become slightly 'nervous' in the faster Riley version of the following year.)

With its new pressed steel bodywork and unusual shape, the Minor has often been compared to the Volkswagen (VW) Beetle, designed before the war by Dr Ferdinand Porsche and developed afterwards. Many Minor enthusiasts consider that it should have attained a similar immortality, though towards the end of production sales showed a severe decline in the face of pressure from more modern cars. Against the 1.6 million Minors of all types, when production stopped in 1971, VW had manufactured 15 million Beetles. The Minor design was, though, in almost every respect superior to the Volkswagen. In the Beetle, the overhanging rear engine contributed to 'tail happy' handling, which was compounded by the treacherous swing axle rear suspension. The air-cooled flat four engine was noisy, and the 'fastback' body, designed in accordance with incorrect aerodynamic theory, gave an unnecessarily cramped interior. By contrast, the Minor was entirely practical, comparatively roomy for the time, and free of vices in its road behaviour. In spite of the numerous poor design features, the Beetle succeeded because of high build quality, good corrosion resistance and reliability. The Minor was, in conception, a much better car, but the experience of users seemed to imply that it was not engineered to the same standard as its German counterpart. (To a great extent, the unreliability of British cars in this era derived from the poor quality of the electrical equipment – dynamos and ignition equipment – which was fitted.) The great boast of Beetle owners was that their cars always started, however cold or damp the day.

After the Minor entered production, two experimental variants were developed which were to have a significant bearing on the evolution of the Mini. The more important was a front-wheel drive Minor, which was an extension of Issigonis's thinking. (In 1964, in a preface to *The Mini Story* by Laurence Pomeroy, he wrote 'The Morris Minor was among the first small cars to be designed nose-heavy and, logically, this concept requires front-wheel drive but I did not know how to do this at that time. Since then, however, I have accumulated sufficient experience to solve this problem, hence *The Mini Story*.'[25]

Thanks to the wide engine compartment, it was possible to make the front-wheel drive Minor quite cheaply, for experimental purposes, by turning a standard engine transversely while still retaining the normal arrangement of clutch and gearbox in line with the crankshaft. One design difficulty which appeared was the provision of drive couplings at the wheels. A normal 'universal' joint (also known as the Hooke or Cardan joint) is unsuitable for steered wheels. At large angular deflections, the velocity of the output side varies, giving a regular thumping sensation and kick-back through the wheel. In addition, the efficiency of power transmission decreases, making the joint liable to failure, since high torque (through use of the low gears) often occurs at the same time as the full steering lock is employed. In the front-wheel drive Minor this was overcome by using modified 'sliding Cardan' joints. These were comparatively large, and since they had to be placed on the effective turning axis of the wheels, determined the diameter of the wheel hubs and bearings. Larger brake drums were also required and the resulting size of this assembly led to the conclusion that the arrangement was impractical for production. However, the road behaviour of the car was thought extremely impressive, and confirmed that front-wheel drive would offer considerable advantages to the ordinary motorist, as soon as the engineering problems could be solved.

The second experimental Minor was an example which was fitted with Moulton rubber suspension, at about the time Issigonis was leaving Morris in 1952. Alex Moulton was successfully using a process for bonding rubber permanently to steel, which enabled him to design various new types of spring that could be used in vehicle applications. The best known was the 'Flexitor', which employed a sleeve of rubber, twisted in torsion. Thanks to its light weight and small size, compared to conventional steel units, it quickly found widespread application for caravans and trailers. Moulton has written of this period

'At the time, my ambition was to get it adopted for motor car suspensions. It was inevitable that I should meet Alec Issigonis, which happened in 1949, and we were to become friends and collaborators in many projects over the years, and I learnt much from this master of mechanical design. He had just launched his Morris Minor with its steel torsion bar front suspension with which he was rightly well satisfied. Knowing that these would not get disturbed in the life of the car, I nevertheless entered into a research programme with Morris to establish the endurance validity of my designs of rubber springs. . . . This was splendidly confirmed at the proving ground. I regarded this test as the "key experiment" on rubber suspension.'[26]

The crucial demonstration was the survival of the rubber units for over 1000 miles (1609 km) on test, on the pavé track at the Motor Industry Research Association (MIRA). This exceeded the fatigue life of many conventional suspensions, and showed clearly that rubber was a practical and durable engineering material.

The strands of development represented by these two Minors were eventually to come to fruition together in Issigonis's next popular car, the Mini.

RDI ARCHIVE

Issigonis at work. The only image which has come to light of him during the period at Alvis.

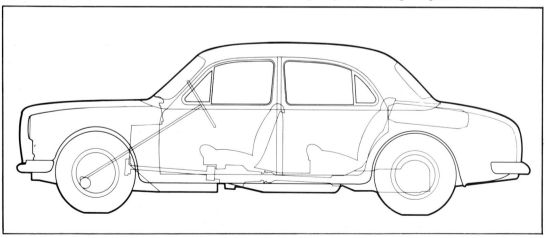

No photograph of the Issigonis-designed Alvis has ever been discovered. This outline has been re-created from original drawings in the possession of Chris Kingham, engine designer on the project.

The Alvis Era – an Interlude

With the Minor established as a convincing success, Issigonis's prestige within Morris was high, and his decision to move in 1952 to Alvis, a relatively small-scale manufacturer, must have seemed strange. Before the war Alvis had built up an enviable reputation as a maker of high quality cars with good performance but restrained appearance. They also made outright sports cars – although these were sports cars for gentlemen, rather than cads! The war had deflected the company into military production and, though when it finished the company returned to limited car production, they found that they were still getting enough orders for armoured cars to keep their production facilities fully occupied. This was financially more secure than making motor cars, as the history of the industry continually shows, but Managing Director John Parkes wanted to revive the reputation for building fine cars. The automobile design profession in Britain was small, and Issigonis had become known as an original talent. He was offered the tempting opportunity to create a completely new design, including the engine, and moved to Coventry to head a small design team – just two other designers and very few assistants.

Issigonis was glad to leave Cowley in the light of the Austin–Morris merger that was taking place that year. Austin was run by the tough-minded Leonard Lord, who had departed as managing director from Morris before the war. The relationship between Leonard Lord and Lord Nuffield had become strained, and shortly afterwards, Lord had joined arch-rival Sir Herbert Austin. Perhaps this background explained the methods of the merger, for there was a feeling that Austin, with Leonard Lord still at the helm, was out to put the Morris people in their place. (The merger, according to Stephen Bayley, was 'an ugly fit, a bit like a train crash'.)[27] Perhaps it is also relevant that in 1936, following the rift with Lord Nuffield, Lord had promised 'I'm going to take that business at Cowley apart, brick by bloody brick.'[28] Alex Moulton believes Issigonis left at the point of merger because 'creative people cannot thrive in a hostile environment'.[29] Issigonis sensed the 'management wars' ahead and has often said 'I'm not a politician, I'm an engineer.' The Alvis project provided a timely escape.

The new Alvis which evolved by 1954 was particularly light and compact, weighing only 22 cwt (1.12 t) with a length of 13 feet (3.96 m). However, it had the Issigonis hallmark of roominess, and was a full five-seater. It was capable of 110 mph (177 kph), and was tested by Issigonis and two of the design team at MIRA, covering 1000 miles (1609 km) a night for a week. The car had an exciting specification for its day: an aluminium 3.5 litre overhead camshaft V8 engine, with cylinder banks set at 90 degrees for minimum vibration. The unusual transmission was by a two-speed gear in the back axle, but an overdrive could be engaged in each gear, giving four effective ratios. The overdrive unit was fitted behind the engine and was very compact, eliminating the usual gearbox bulge in the floor which tended to encroach into the foot-wells. The idea was that in town the gearbox would be in 'low', and rapid changes would be made on the electrically operated overdrive. On the open road high ratio would be chosen, and switching the overdrive in or out would provide enough flexibility for most road situations. The suspension also was novel, using the rubber springs developed by Alex Moulton.

The Lightweight Special hillclimb car had once again exercised an influence on Issigonis's career at this point, for it was through David Fry, who had also built and raced his own hillclimb special, the Freikaiserwagen, that

Issigonis came in 1949 to meet Alex Moulton, a friend and near neighbour of Fry's. It was an unconnected but intriguing coincidence that Issigonis had himself already used rubber as a suspension medium, in the Lightweight Special, though in this case the rubber was used in the form of loops in tension. Moulton used it, initially, in torsion. Subsequently he designed units for production cars using rubber in compression and shear.

The Moulton family firm, at Bradford on Avon, had for many years manufactured simple rubber rings for the buffers of railway rolling stock. Alex Moulton believed that the material could find a wider use in engineering applications. For example, the 'Flexitor' unit he devised became widely used in caravans and for trailer applications, while the experimental rubber-sprung Morris Minor vindicated his faith in the durability of rubber for the suspension of cars. He went on to design a spring called the 'Diabolo', resembling a pair of rubber cones, working in compression.[30] This was the design which attracted Issigonis for use in the new Alvis. The new spring offered high load-bearing capacity for light weight; it was compact; it had desirable rising-rate characteristics, and it possessed a significant degree of self-damping.

After initial experiments with the Alvis, it became apparent to Issigonis and Moulton that these hollow conical rubber springs could also be used to displace a water-based fluid from their inner side under compression, and that this effect could be used to interlink the front and rear suspension hydraulically. Citroën had already achieved interconnection on the 2CV with coil springs, and the startling new DS, with self-levelling oleo-preumatic suspension, was about to be revealed. Moulton recorded 'the notion of interconnection was being much discussed in the tiny coterie of engineers who are concerned with such things – and how few they are!' The effect of interconnection is that when a front wheel encounters a bump, a certain volume of fluid is displaced into the rear spring unit, and simultaneously raises the rear suspension. When the rear wheel hits the bump, the same process happens in reverse. In effect, the interconnection averages out the pitch imparted to the car when encountering a bump. The experiment was successful, and Moulton recalled 'I shall always remember the impression of ride luxury when we first interconnected that Alvis.'[31]

This interconnected system was the origin of the Hydrolastic system, as fitted to the BMC 1100 and later Minis. The system gives the effect of softer springing in the 'pitch mode' because, in a sense, the compliance of front and rear springs can both be used to accommodate the rise of an individual wheel to a bump. Moreover, it achieves this softening effect without the usual concomitant undesirable characteristic of soft springs – excessive body roll when cornering, which interferes with accurate steering, both through geometrical suspension effects and through disturbing the driver's control. The reason is that when the car rolls under the influence of cornering forces, both front and rear springs attempt to displace fluid simultaneously, which manifestly they cannot do. The result is a suspension which can be made soft in pitch for comfort, but which stiffens up dramatically in corners, giving accurate control of the body motion and good control. The only drawback of the system is that on a very bumpy, or corrugated surface, (the 'bounce mode'), both front and rear wheels may be attempting to displace fluid at the same time, leading to a very choppy and perhaps unacceptably hard ride. (Later 'Hydragas' cars did not suffer from this defect.)

In spite of the pioneering technology of the car, Alvis management eventually decided not to put it into production. The investment required was considerable, and it was felt that the funds would be better expended on the aero-engine and armoured car business where demand was steady, and orders scheduled well ahead. A periodic downturn in the market for new cars occurred at the time that the decision was being reached, and this underlined the risky nature of the business. Issigonis commented 'When we came to consider the cost of tooling . . . it was out of the question for a firm of that size. There were so many problems, perhaps it was just as well it never happened, and in a way I was relieved when Sir Leonard Lord rang me one day in late 1955 and said: "Come back to Longbridge".'[32] Alvis destroyed the prototype car, along with all the drawings, and at the time of writing no photograph or snapshot has yet been discovered.

As well as his professed functionalism, Issigonis can also display attributes of the idealistic designer, only partly responsive to the needs of a major company, for this was not the first time production economics had come between his design and its realisation. It is arguable that his best work was always done when he was subject to a powerful managerial overlord.

When Issigonis returned to the mainstream car business from his self-imposed exile at Alvis, the merger between Austin and Morris had become a reality, and as Issigonis had perhaps feared, it had been far from tranquil. There had been a definite desire on the part of Austin management to show the Morris people that things were now going to be done *their* way. Company Chairman Leonard Lord was a determined man, now firmly in control of the new British Motor Corporation (BMC). He was, though, a highly experienced and astute motor industry man, with a thorough grounding in production technology, and had himself been a first-rate jig and tool draughtsman. Lord recog-

nised that Austin–Morris had a model range that was ageing badly, particularly in the important 1.5 litre sector, where the Austin Cambridge was now looking decidedly old-fashioned. He had identified Issigonis as the man to create a new medium-sized car and resolved to woo him back from Alvis. In fact, Issigonis seems to have been the only designer in the British motor industry to whom Lord would entrust a project of this importance for the new organisation. 'He'd have torn the world apart to get him', considers Alex Moulton.[33] For his part, Issigonis recorded 'I was glad to be back with Lord – a tough, wonderful man with a fantastic personality, a born businessman and a great production engineer.'[34]

Issigonis began work on the new family car at Longbridge in 1956. It was to have conventional rear-wheel drive, and to be powered by a four-cylinder engine derived from the Alvis project – in effect, half of the V8. It was also unusual in having a single, central hydro-elastic 'spring' with pipe connections to each wheel. (The experiment proved unsuccessful.) However, the Suez invasion that September and the resulting oil embargo quickly changed priorities within BMC. Leonard Lord observed the spate of 'bubble' cars that rapidly grew in popularity and decided that the company must go all out to produce a small economy vehicle – but one that was also a real car. He decreed that all design work on the new family car was to stop in order to create this economy car in just two years. In a sense, the 'Mini' was to be a replay of the production of the original Austin Seven: a cheap but 'proper' small car would be engineered to take sales from the marginal baby cars. His idea found a ready audience with Issigonis.

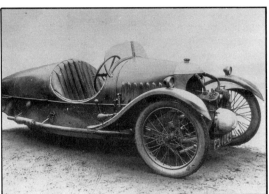

The spirit of the cyclecar. Spindly, quick, great fun, but not the true ancestor of the popular small car. (A three-wheeler Morgan in the 1920s.)

The car that changed everything. Four seats, four cylinders, four wheel brakes. The Austin Seven, introduced in 1922, was a true miniature car. This example is from 1925.

Background to the Mini – the Evolution of the Mini-car

Though his name is inseparable from the Mini, Issigonis did not invent the mini-car formula. Throughout automotive history, from the earliest days, there were attempts to produce compact, low-cost cars. Before the First World War, when motor cars were generally powerful and stately playthings for the rich, some enthusiasts were building 'cyclecars', intended to have a more popular appeal. Even the famous De Dion Boutons launched in the last years of the 19th century, which did so much to make France (and, by diffusion, the rest of Europe) automobile-minded, were little more than motorised tricycles and quadricycles.

This was the problem with the cyclecar. As the name suggested, it was firmly rooted in the cycle and motorcycle industries. Every effort was made to build vehicles of minimum weight and at minimum cost, but cycle technology proved not to transfer well to four-wheeled transport. 'Proper' Edwardian motor cars were in fact substantially built and surprisingly reliable. The cyclecars were spindly and erratic, though often, as with the British GN, capable of a remarkable turn of speed – the 1921 'Coupe des Cyclecars' at Boulogne was run over a circuit of ordinary roads, the winning GN averaging 66 mph (96.5 kph). The simple, light, air-cooled engines which proved quite adequate when installed in motorcycles were required to run for longer at high power when driving a four-wheeled chassis, and the skimpy bodywork that was fitted added to the load. The engines overheated, seized and wore out. Road shocks stressed and broke the frames and suspensions. Clutch and transmission failures were a constant headache.

Many manufacturers were anxious to avoid the expense and weight of a true gearbox, and tried ingenious solutions such as variable ratio friction drive, or multiple chains, but few proved durable. After the war there was a great upsurge in popular enthusiasm for motoring, and in the 1920s the cyclecar industry enjoyed a minor boom. (It is an interesting aside on the evolution of the mini-car that both world wars brought in their wake a major boost for powered road transport, especially in the economy sector.)

In 1922 came the car that changed everything – the Austin Seven. At a stroke it made the cyclecars look like antiques, for it was a true miniature car. It had a four-cylinder water-cooled engine, not a modified motorcyle power unit, and a conventional clutch and transmission. It could boast saloon bodywork (few cyclecars could carry the weight of closed coachwork), four-wheel brakes and sold for only £100. The spidery cyclecar was dead; the compact Austin Seven became the examplar for a new type of miniature car, which offered a similar mechanical specification to its bigger brethren. Three hundred thousand Austin Sevens were made in 14 years and licences to build them were taken out in Germany (by BMW), France, and the USA. In Japan, Datsun (now Nissan) started in the motor business by building an Austin Seven copy.

In the wake of the success of the Austin Seven, many other companies attempted to improve on the habitability of the miniature car. From the 1930s onward, the general move away from coachwork built on a separate chassis, towards unitary pressed steel contruction helped save weight, lower the height of the car and improve roominess. Many designers also felt that integration of the engine with the gearbox and final drive (the 'differential') was essential. Aggregating these three components into one saved space, and further improved the interior of the car by removing the bulky transmission tunnel. In addition, the manufacturing process was eased by the possibility of building the engine and transmission together and offering the assembly up complete to the bodyshell, and there was also a considerable weight saving. The question was where to place this combined engine/drive-train.

At Fiat, Dante Giacosa believed it should be at the rear, and after the Second World War produced some extremely ingenious cars such as the Nuove Cinquecento, which offered remarkable accommodation within its tiny overall dimensions. In fact the rear engine was a widespread post-war trend, and to the designer offered the attractions of roominess and low noise. Against the concept is the rearward weight distribution, which makes forgiving handling in corners difficult to achieve, while the cars are hard to engineer to the same level of crash safety as front-engined models. Not with-standing these objections, several successful rear-engined models were produced following the war, notably the Volkswagen Beetle, which had its roots in Dr Ferdinand Porsche's pre-war design study for a popular car, and the morphologically similar Renault 4CV. However, the industry soon returned to the front-engined layout, and at the time of writing, practically the only European companies making rear-engined cars are Skoda (in Czechoslovakia), and Porsche, with the 911 sports car. (This does not include the various special high performance cars such as Ferrari and Lamborghini, which have mid-mounted engines. These do not suffer from the disadvantage of unfavourable weight distribution, and their balance is close to the ideal.)

In Sweden, a car emerged after the war that was to prove remarkably prescient in its conception. In 1945 the Saab aeroplane company anticipated a lull in post-war aircraft demand, and began planning the production of a small car. Perhaps because the team was unfamiliar with established automobile industry practice, the little Saab arrived at one step with various modern features that economy models from the rest of the industry were to acquire only piecemeal. It had a unitary pressed steel body, hydraulic brakes and front-wheel drive. The choice of a cheap-to-build two-stroke engine proved an unfortunate blind alley, but the Saab showed that front-wheel drive was sufficiently practical to be incorporated in a small car, and the company's many rally successes also helped to show that the roadholding and driveability were of a high order.

The concept of front-wheel drive is virtually as old as the motor industry, though in Europe the system did not get major publicity until the Tracta cars built by J A Grégoire ran at Le Mans from 1927. At about the same time the respected Alvis company produced a range of competition

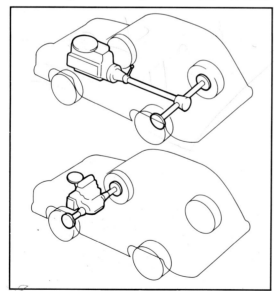

Rear-wheel and front-wheel drive. The integration of engine, gearbox and differential gives a considerable improvement in passenger space.

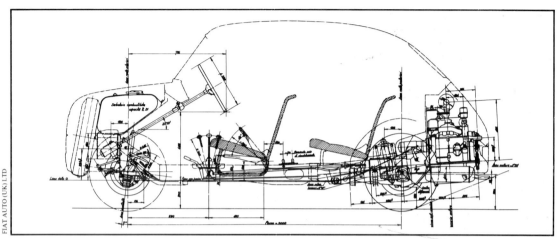

FIAT AUTO (UK) LTD

Integration of the drive train did not dictate a front engine and front-wheel drive. Engineer Dante Giacosa at Fiat believed that placing the engine in the rear was the most economical and effective solution. This detailed 1953 drawing of the Fiat 600 shows how the rear engine/transmission package liberates passenger space.

NATIONAL MOTOR MUSEUM

Not all rear-engined cars were optimised for interior volume. The Volkswagen Beetle is relatively cramped for its size, having been styled in the light of incorrect aerodynamic theories.

Similar objections to the Beetle apply to the post-war Renault 4CV. Volkswagen inventor Ferdinand Porsche is said to have worked on the Renault project, during post-war captivity in France.

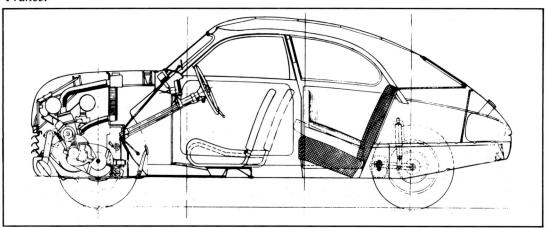

Launched in 1949, the Saab 92 was another victim of fastback aerodynamic styling, but it demonstrated that front-wheel drive was an effective solution in smaller, utility cars and could provide first-class road behaviour.

and road cars in England. The main objection to the system was one of serviceability. As the reliability of individual components was not very good, it made good sense to have engine, clutch, gearbox and differential 'strung out', as it were, linearly along the car, to allow individual replacement. Front-wheel drive tended to require that the whole engine/drive-train assembly needed lifting out to rectify faults. However, as we have seen, there was also an independent move towards the 'condensation' of the engine and drive-line in the interests of space-saving and production efficiency during the 1930s and 40s, and this helped achieve one of the pre-conditions for the development of front-wheel drive in small cars.

There were also engineering problems to be solved, chiefly associated with driving through the steered wheels. The drive shafts had to cope with the suspension movements of each front wheel, and also had to allow steering. As described in the chapter on the experimental front-wheel drive Minor, ordinary Hooke or universal joints are not able to transmit power smoothly through these high steering angles, and special constant velocity joints had to be evolved.

Probably the greatest propaganda for front-wheel drive was created by Citroën's remarkable Traction Avant, introduced in 1934. Its acceptance was helped by other modern features, such as a chassis-less pressed steel body (André Citroën visited the USA to obtain press tools from the famous Budd company, and to obtain help in getting the design into production), but in the public mind the key to the success of the car was front-wheel drive. This tradition was carried on post-war with the remarkable DS, which looked quite extraordinarily futuristic when first shown in 1955, and with the other Citroën models, such as the Deux Chevaux (2CV). It is significant that Issigonis was a great admirer of Citroën engineering. 'We had them at the factory', Jack Daniels recalled, 'Issigonis loved Citroëns . . . the most advanced car in the world at the time.'[35]

This was the technical background to the progress towards front-wheel drive, and to the reduction in the space taken up by the mechanical parts, when Issigonis returned to the mainstream car business from his voluntary exile at Alvis.

The greatest propaganda for front-wheel drive: the Citröen Traction Avant.

The production Mini – as you could buy it in 1960.

Issigonis Tackles the Mini Problem

'God damn these bloody awful bubble-cars. We must drive them off the streets by designing a proper miniature car.'[36] According to Issigonis's recollection, this was the remark of Leonard Lord that initiated the Mini project.

Demand for cheap travel after the Second World War had led to a resurgence of low-cost vehicles, artisan-built by a variety of small firms. These were often three-wheelers, like the Reliant, and appealed because they could be driven on motorcyle licences and attracted lower rates of duty. Some, like the Bond, had small single-cylinder two-stroke engines of motorcycle origin, and in some respects they were analogous to the cyclecars that sprang up after the First World War. Perhaps the movement would have died as the motoring public became more sophisticated, but the Suez crisis in 1956, and the first 'oil shock' which resulted, gave microcars a new boost. (In the aftermath of Suez, petrol was rationed from between 6 to 10.5 gallons per month, depending on engine capacity).

Alex Moulton recalls driving to meet Issigonis at the Welcome Hotel, Stratford-upon-Avon, during that post-Suez winter in a Heinkel three-wheeler bubble car with a 175 cc engine. ('Simply a device for getting 60 miles to the gallon.') Issigonis viewed it with disdain, joking 'Leonard Lord wants me to design an economy car. Whatever it is, it won't have one cylinder and three wheels. It's going to have four wheels

Reliant Regal, 1954.

Left: *Isetta 'bubble car'. 'Simply a device for getting 60 miles to the gallon.' But not all bubble cars were, in Leonard Lord's words, 'bloody awful'.* Right: *The Messerschmitt was built to very high standards, though one had to sacrifice a considerable amount of comfort.*

and four cylinders.'[37]

When, early in 1957, it was decided to put aside the 1.5 litre family saloon project, Issigonis was free to concentrate entirely on the urgent development of the new small car. He intended that it was not merely to be an economy car, but like the Morris Minor should set new standards for comfort and habitability. Not only that, but the suspension and road behaviour were to be in advance of conventional saloons of normal size. (Indeed, in the event, it proved to out-handle specialist sports cars.) There were echoes of Morris Minor production planning too, when Lord told Issigonis, 'You can use any engine you like, so long as we have it on our present production lines.'[38]

Very demanding constraints sometimes provoke the most creative design solutions. In some cases it may simply be cost. For the Mini, it was the arbitrary target of designing a car to be no more than 10 feet (3.04 m) in length that Issigonis set himself. Approximately 8'6" (2.58 m) of this length was to be used to seat four adults without undue contortions, in acceptable comfort and with room for luggage. The engine and drive-train would have to fit into the remaining 18 inches (0.44 m)!

In March 1957, as the programme gathered way, Issigonis 'grabbed Jack Daniels and took him up to Longbridge'. As on the Minor project, Daniels was to be the right-hand man, turning most of Issigonis's sketches into working drawings, and running the project on a day-to-day basis. Also on the team were Chris Kingham, engine man on the Alvis project, and Charles Griffin, a development engineer from Cowley. 'These cars weren't designed in vast offices; there were maybe six people and a couple of fitters', former BMC engineer Ron Unsworth recalled. 'Issigonis would be the first to admit he wasn't an administrator; he liked to build up "The Cell", a compact unit he could control. He

would say that the purpose of the small group was "to make as many mistakes as possible, as quickly and cheaply as possible".'[39]

The picture of Issigonis that emerges here is of a man who was not remotely interested in industrial hierarchies and organisational structures. The project itself was the all-important thing. At the same time, he did not welcome too much initiative from members of the team. 'He was the designer', says Unsworth, 'and we were there to do things *his* way.'[40] In another man, this attitude might have alienated his assistants, but Issigonis had the respect of his associates through his obvious talents and mental agility. ('Life was never dull.'[41]) 'The thing that impressed me', Unsworth says, 'is that he was really fantastic at sketching. He would do a sketch in your presence, and convey exactly what he wanted.'[42] It seems that for Issigonis, sketching with pencil and paper was not done to explore possible solutions; his drawings were to communicate his intentions to the group. The actual design work was internalised, at some level of Issigonis's mentality, and seemed already to exist, in a remarkably complete form, before he put pencil to paper. In *Morris Minor* (1981), Paul Skilleter suggested 'Looking at these sketches today, one has the feeling that Issigonis was drawing from life, from solid objects which he could see in front of him'. Those who worked on his projects have found that a precise description.

His attitude to his assistants is confirmed by all of them who have recalled those days. John Sheppard, who had come with Issigonis from the Alvis team says 'He was very domineering. He knew what he wanted. "Now go away and *do* it." If you argued with him, he didn't want to know. If you thought, well, he's wrong, but I'm going to *prove* to him he's wrong, he would accept it in the end. But mainly he was right.'[43]

Issigonis decided that the new compact car

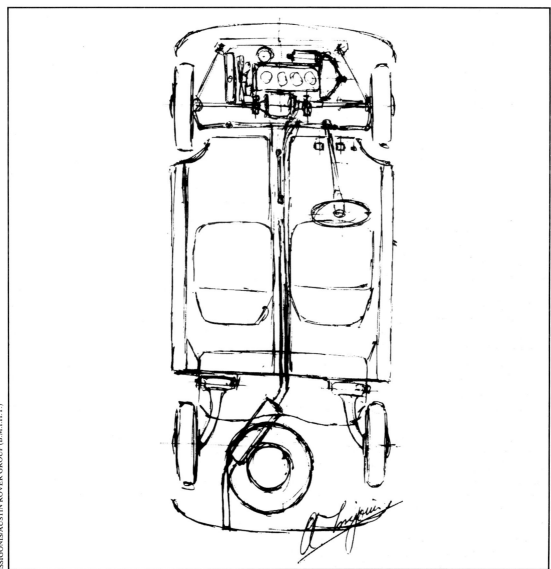

This sketch plan of the Mini by Issigonis illustrates how wheel size determines the intrusion of the wheel arch into the foot wells. It also shows the benefit derived from placing the gearbox under the engine.

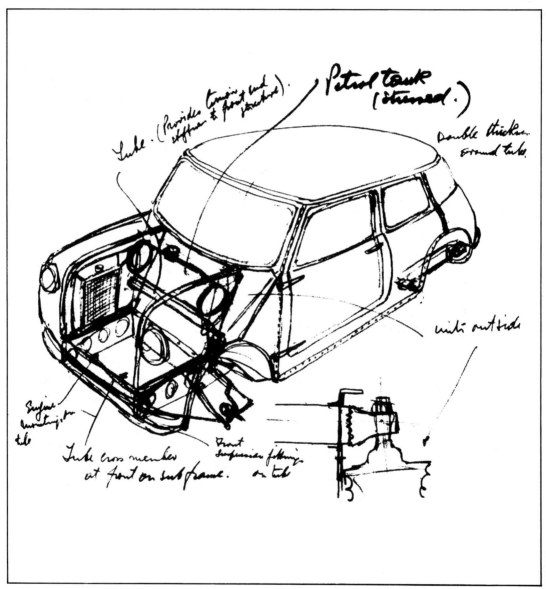

Issigonis's drawings were done to communicate his intentions to the group. This is an early version of the Mini, with the petrol tank under the bonnet.

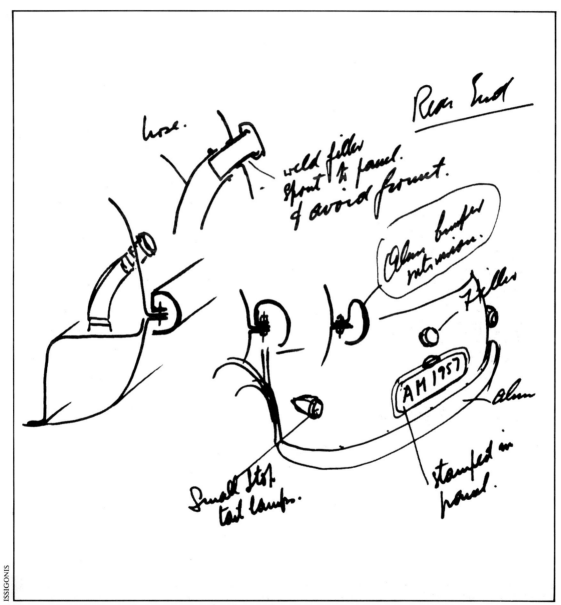

Sketches exploring a later rear-mounted petrol tank and methods of assembly.

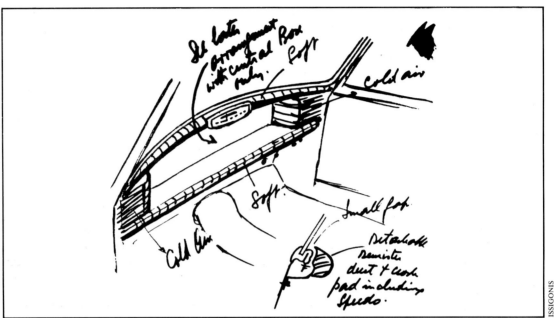

ISSIGONIS

As with the Morris Minor, Issigonis defined the dash and interior in great detail. Below: *Sketches for an engine mounting.*

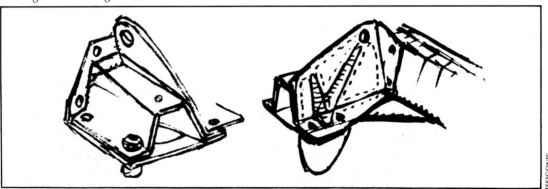

ISSIGONIS

Right: *Surprisingly, the distinctive Mini shape was not created specially for the new BMC economy car project. This is XC9001, the prototype of the mid-sized rear-wheel drive 1.5 litre family saloon created by Issigonis and his team on his return from Alvis in 1956. The Mini was almost a simple scaled-down XC9001, although the bonnet is proportionately shorter. This scaling process may, in part, have suggested the adoption of unusually small wheels for the Mini.*

would be front-wheel drive. Jack Daniels believes that the prototype front-wheel drive, transverse engine Morris Minor Issigonis had designed earlier (but apparently never drove, owing to his move to Alvis) had important propaganda value within the BMC management. At that time the idea was considered radical by the conservative British motor industry, which had shied away from this and other features, such as rear engines, air-cooled engines and fully independent suspension, all of which were common on the Continent. However, the front-wheel drive Minor spent much of its life parked under Managing Director George Harriman's window, and in the severe winter of 1955–56, Daniels had to drive regularly between Cowley, Longbridge, and Hasely Manor, near Warwick, where BMC was developing four-wheel drive military vehicles. In view of the ice and snow, he would use the front-wheel drive Minor, saying 'I'm taking the safest vehicle we've got',[44] and became thoroughly convinced

of its handling virtues. The management was also aware of their engineers' evaluation of the competition and of the front-wheel drive Citroëns that were at the factory for this purpose. 'We must have front drive on the new car', Daniels told Issigonis, when the Mini project got underway.[45]

This certainly accorded with the way Issigonis's design thinking had developed. The absence of a transmission tunnel would also ease the accommodation problem in the tiny car, while a transversely mounted engine would fit into the almost absurdly small space Issigonis had allowed himself. Of course he could have located the condensed engine and transmission package at the rear, as in Giacosa's clever Fiats, but his own experience as a driver – one who had designed, built and driven his own competition car – weighed against adopting an inherently unbalanced set-up.

Initial experiments centred around a two-cylinder unit, derived from the Austin 'A'-series

THE AUSTIN ROVER GROUP (B.M.I.H.T.)

engine, as then fitted to production Morris Minors and Austin A35 and A40s. This had the advantage that it was short enough, with clutch and gearbox fitted directly on to the end, to be accommodated in the engine bay, but power was too low, and the engine too rough. It was decided early on to find a way to fit in the full four-cylinder unit. Issigonis proposed putting the gearbox below the engine, driven by a gear-train, and integrated into one structure, to achieve minimum size. One consequence was that engine and gearbox would share the same oil – a condition that made some engineers apprehensive. The fear was that coarse debris and metallic chips from the gearbox would compromise engine life. The fact that this solution

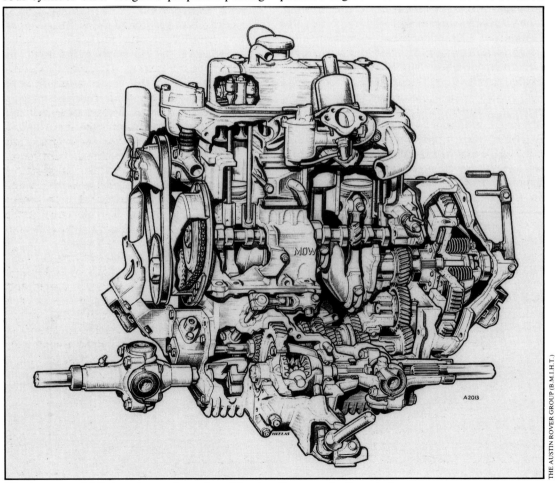

The integrated Mini engine and gearbox 'sharing the same bath water'.

had not been tried before was no deterrent to Issigonis ('An expert is someone who tells you why you can't do something'),[46] and so the engine and gearbox came, in his phrase, 'to share the same bath water'.

With the Minor, Issigonis had explored the benefit of smaller wheels to the habitability of the car. With the Mini, it would be even more crucial to reduce the intrusion of the wheel arches into the living space. 'We fought for every quarter inch' said a team member, and so Issigonis proposed to go even smaller – to ten inch rims, though at the time only lightweight bubble cars had run on such small tyres. The Dunlop Company was prepared to co-operate in developing the necessary tyres, but this decision of Issigonis's was even more daring than amalgamating the engine and gearbox. If mechanical problems had occurred, a 'fix' could no doubt have been found. If the tyre programme had failed, the project could probably not have been salvaged. The whole body design, steering-gear and suspension would have needed to be completely changed. In fact, the labour-intensive task of drawing up all the sheet metal parts for production proceeded on the assumption that the tyres would be available.

For the suspension, a space-saving solution was already at hand. The system evolved by Alex Moulton, using rubber in compression, and already tried by Issigonis and Moulton at Alvis, was well suited to the tightly packaged Mini. At the rear, the links could be contrived to run horizontally under the car, giving independent suspension, with virtually no intrusion of springs or dampers into the passenger or luggage space. The suspension was crucial to the project – both in endowing the car with excellent road manners, and in maximising passenger space. 'Don't separate Moulton from the Mini achievement',[47] comments Daniels.

These Moulton rubber springs had the desir-able property of variable rate (stiffening as load increases) – an essential quality in such a tiny car, since the variation in load (from driver only to four people) is a much greater proportion of total all-up weight than in conventionally sized vehicles. This design problem can be visualised by considering that a 2 ton Bentley may also be driven with the driver alone, or with four people. The difference in this case, as a proportion of the total weight carried by the Bentley's suspension, is rather small. But in the Mini, this variation is about 30 per cent. The suspension must be equally efficient at either loading, so the lighter a four-seat car is built, the more difficult, in some respects, suspension design becomes.

The original intention was to couple the front and rear pairs of springs on each side by fluid connection. (Moulton opines that Issigonis had 'smelled blood with the coupled suspension on the Alvis', so good was it in controlling pitch.) However, this system was not completed in time, and the Mini was manufactured with simple uncoupled rubber springs (the 'dry cone Mini') until 1964, when 'Hydrolastic' suspension was introduced.

In this period, Issigonis was driving the Mini project with great passion. He met and talked tirelessly with friends who were informed and interested in car design. Whenever at the Dowsons' farm he would talk to George about the Mini. Jack Daniels remembers Issigonis, Moulton, and John Morris, Chief Engineer at SU Carburettors 'being always in conversation. They were the Three Musketeers'.[48]

The team worked at an extraordinary rate, vindicating Issigonis's faith in a small, compact group. Seven months after the project started, two running prototypes were produced. Leonard Lord's backing had been vital. The team was given a priority number for parts manufacture, and 'everything stopped when they saw that number on a drawing'. The machine shop would make a part overnight, from a freehand sketch, if it was dimensioned.

The two prototypes gave invaluable information, covering many miles over Cotswold roads in disguised form. The tests revealed that the forward-facing carburettor could ice up, that the gear stick could conduct noise into the passenger compartment, and that there was a problem in restraining the engine under reaction torque. (This latter problem is far worse in a front-wheel drive car, since there is no driven rear axle to share the torque reaction through its own mountings.) The tests also showed that the baby car was incredibly fast – too fast in fact, being timed at 92 mph (148 kph).

For production models it was decided to remove the carburettor from the cold airflow by rotating the engine through 180 degrees, and another coupling gear was inserted between engine and gearbox to correct the direction of rotation. This reduced the efficiency of power transmission by about four per cent, but as another curb on top speed, the engine capacity was reduced by 100 cc from the original capacity of 948 cc. In a remarkable parallel to the Morris Minor programme, a late decision was also made to widen the car by 2 inches, though it appears that the spur for this was to increase the space, rather than to adjust the appearance. The combined effect of these three measures was to cut the speed of production Minis to 74 mph – a more reasonable figure for the tyres and road conditions of the day.

Sir Leonard Lord made his first run in one of the prototypes in July 1958. After a mere five minute drive round the works he turned to

THE AUSTIN ROVER GROUP (B.M.I.H.T.)

One of the two Mini prototypes, with a modified Austin A35 radiator as disguise.

Issigonis, saying 'Alec, this is it. I want it in production within twelve months.'[49]

The Mini was finally unveiled in August 1959 to tremendous public interest. Our eyes have now become attuned to the size and shape of Minis and their derivatives, and it is difficult to recapture the sense of just how different the car seemed. In fact it appeared extraordinary in comparison to conventional small cars; many people made expeditions to their local dealers simply to view the new creation.

The shape, of course, was so unusual because Issigonis again had complete control of the exterior design. According to Jack Daniels, 'Pinin' Farina was shown a pre-production example by BMC management, and asked for

THE AUSTIN ROVER GROUP (B.M.I.H.T)

Mini prototype showing the original orientation of the engine. The front-facing carburettor was prone to icing, so for production the engine was turned round to remove the intake from the cold airflow. The prototypes were two inches narrower than production cars.

his view. 'Don't touch it – it's unique' was his comment. Daniels confirms Issigonis's complete authority over the design. 'The Mini shape was Issigonis full stop. Make no mistake; that shape was Issigonis.'[50] The exterior reflected the functional mind that designed it (for example, there were external flanges where body panels joined together, for ease of welding), and Issigonis's uncompromising view that 'If you style a car, it goes out of date.'[51] When his friend Laurence Pomeroy, a distinguished motoring journalist, pointed out that however much he might dislike the fact, many buyers rated styling above functional qualities like economy, ease of parking and cornering power, Issigonis replied 'Yes, my dear Pom, I know there are tens of thousands of such people, but I will not design cars for them!'[52]

From the inside, the functional philosophy behind the car was even more apparent. Simple lanyards were fitted to open the doors. There were no wind-up windows – the glass slid back and forth in tracks. Deletion of the winder mechanism meant that at the bottom of the doors there were capacious pockets for storage. (They accommodated, Issigonis quipped, the ingredients to make perfect Dry Martinis: 27 bottles of gin and one of Vermouth!) Instead of a dashboard, the instruments were condensed into a simple central binnacle, which comprised a speedometer and various warning lights. Beneath it was a wide, deep and practical parcel shelf. There was, however, no designated location for a radio – Issigonis didn't like them.

The use of front-wheel drive in a popular car caused great interest. The informed public wanted to know, in particular, how this would affect the cornering characteristics. In a rear-wheel drive car, cornering on slippery surfaces may lead to the back of the car sliding outwards. This is partly due to the fact that the rear tyres are being required to do two jobs – to provide a lateral cornering force, and to transmit power to the road. The driver's response must be to reduce the steering lock (extending even to the use of 'opposite lock' in extreme situations), and to ease off the accelerator. Many drivers find that this two-part action becomes instinctive, but a body of opinion maintains that it is counter-intuitive for the unskilled driver. This school of thought considers that front-wheel drive offers greater safety, for if the front wheels begin to slide out, the instinctive reaction is to lift the foot off the accelerator and this restores some of the cornering power to the front wheels, causing the car to tighten its line in the desired direction.

However, the good road behaviour of the Mini was not due solely to this property of front-wheel drive. There was also the general suspension design, including the rising-rate characteristics of the rubber springs, low body-roll, and precise rack and pinion steering. But though front-wheel drive was novel in Britain, motoring writers and the general public were rapidly convinced of the accuracy and fidelity of the road behaviour of the new car.

In spite of the great public interest and favourable press reports, initial sales of the Mini faltered. Issigonis had believed he was designing for traditional buyers of small economy cars, but these customers, who often did their own maintenance, were wary of the new mechanical layout, believing, perhaps rightly, that the Mini power-train, packed into the tiny under-bonnet space, would lead to more costly and difficult repairs, compared to a traditional rear-wheel drive layout. Curiously, the car caught on rapidly with the more affluent and fashion-conscious sections of society; Lord Snowdon was an early high-profile Mini owner, while Alec Issigonis demonstrated the car in Windsor Park to the Queen. In retrospect though, the company considered that the car 'quivered on the brink of

THE AUSTIN ROVER GROUP (B.M.I.H.T.)

A Mini mock-up in July 1957; a rejected proposal for a wrap-around grille.

THE AUSTIN ROVER GROUP (B.M.I.H.T.)

This 1958 mock-up has the more successful radiator grille of the eventual production Mini.

failure' in its first year of life. There were various problems – the fruit of the somewhat rushed development programme; a sheet metal joint lapped the wrong way in the floor caused the cars to leak water. (The drought conditions of the 1959 summer probably contributed to a failure to notice the problem in pre-production cars.) There was also a problem with oil leaking on to the clutch, causing slippage, and the torque reaction of the engine tended to loosen the mountings, leading to a noisy thumping as the car pulled away. The exhaust system had been designed to assist the engine location, but the loads were higher than expected, and exhaust pipe fractures were a frequent occurrence.

To solve these problems Issigonis did some extra design work, though a lot of the 'trouble shooting' on the production car was done by the team under Jack Daniels. Once the faults were cured, the unique cachet of the car began to win sales; it became, in effect, the 'trendy' (the contemporary adjective) accoutrement for the fashionable Londoner in the 'Swinging Sixties'. The good handling characteristics also allowed the Mini to be tuned for greatly enhanced performance, and a series of rally and competition wins began to prove that it was not merely an economical ugly duckling. However, it remained a predominantly middle-class car (though the buyers themselves regarded it as 'classless' – in other words, the only economy car they were prepared to own). As late as 1977 a British Leyland survey confirmed that this trend still existed and, for internal consumption, characterised Mini buyers as 20 per cent 'Colonel's wife', 20 per cent 'Blimps', and 15 per cent housewives. 'Flat hats' (manual workers) accounted for only 10 per cent of sales.

The Mini was put on sale initially at just under £500 (though the de luxe version, which was the one usually ordered, cost £537). This was a remarkably low price for a vehicle that embodied so many novel features, and it may well have been that BMC missed a chance to put a premium on such striking innovation. Calculating the true profit earned by a car is a difficult task, depending as it does on arcane accounting procedures, but one estimate was that in 1966 each Mini made only about £15 profit. According to another assessment, the operation actually made a loss.

Then there is the oft-told story that when the Mini was launched, the cost-conscious Ford

The Mini as fashionable accoutrement? Marian Faithfull in 1967 at the Rolling Stones' appeal against their drug sentences.

BBC HULTON PICTURE LIBRARY

company took one apart to the last nut, costed every item for production, and decided that they couldn't build it for the price. The story may be apocryphal (though it would be surprising if they had not done something of the kind); in any event, Ford delayed nearly twenty years before introducing their own front-wheel drive 'baby' – the Fiesta. However, these figures are contentious and must be considered in conjunction with other factors. For example BMC hoped, perhaps over-optimistically, that providing a low-cost car for the young first-time buyer would win loyalty to the marque for subsequent larger and more profitable purchases. There is also the question of establishing a high total production volume, thus reducing the cost of items which might be shared in common between Minis and other BMC cars, and thereby contributing to the profitability of the whole range.

The Mini went on sale through the separate Austin and Morris dealerships as the Austin

BBC HULTON PICTURE LIBRARY

Enthusiasts soon discovered Mini handling, as shown here at Brands Hatch. The Mini also distinguished itself by winning the Monte Carlo Rally three times.

Seven and the Mini Minor. Both names were intended to capitalise on earlier successful models from the respective companies. However, these slightly bogus historical resonances were lost on the public, who recognised it as a quite new type of car. It was not a marketing decision, but public usage, that caused the car to become known inevitably as just the 'Mini' – a name that changed the English language, leading to such neologisms as 'mini-skirt', 'mini-

THE AUSTIN ROVER GROUP (B.M.I.H.T.)

The Mini in production.

bar', and even 'mini A-bomb'.

Issigonis's Mini provoked the wider development of a new class of car in imitation, though the reluctance with which other manufacturers followed suit showed that there were high costs in building such a tightly packed assembly of parts. For the consumer, the car was genuinely novel and highly attractive. In production terms it was almost a step too far.

THE AUSTIN ROVER GROUP (B.M.I.H.T.)

Sectioned Mini illustrates how the 'busy' engine compartment allows room in the cabin. The rubber rear springs create virtually no intrusion into the load space.

Production 1100s of 1963 (top) and 1967. The styling lasted well, but the success of the car perhaps made BMC complacent. In the early years the 1100 outsold even the legendary Ford Cortina.

The BMC 1100

Work on the new medium-sized car (the XC 9001) that had brought Issigonis to Longbridge had been completely halted to allow the crash Mini programme. There was, though, an urgent need for a new car in this sector, and rather than return to the original project it was decided to produce a vehicle based on enlarged Mini engineering. The power plant people had succeeded in increasing the capacity of that old workhorse, the 'A'-series engine to 1.1 litres, and hence the '1100' project (known as ADO 16 within the company) was born.

Whereas the Mini was largely created at Long-bridge, the 1100 was more a Cowley project, and though Issigonis as 'technical director' was in overall charge, the chief engineer and man on the spot was Charles Griffin. There was also the involvement of 'Pinin' Farina (established as an Austin consultant since the early 1950s) for the external form. Nevertheless, the 1100 was intended to embody Issigonis's ideals of maximum habitability and excellent road behaviour. Griffin had been development engineer on the Mini project and was thus well trained in the

Battista Pinin Farina (second from left) in 1958 with the fruit of an earlier collaboration – the Austin A40. His son Sergio (far right) did the styling on the Issigonis 1100. Leonard Lord (far left) created BMC and was tough enough to keep it on the right track. George Harriman (second from right) succeeded him as Chairman and Managing Director.

'Issigonis school'. A triumvirate consisting of Issigonis, Griffin, and Moulton was responsible for the engineering of the new car.

The involvement of Farina on the bodywork gave rise to the oft-quoted story that the Italian, knowing Issigonis's work on the Mini and Minor, one day innocently asked if he too considered himself to be a 'stylist'. Drawing himself up to his full height, Issigonis is alleged to have replied icily 'No. I am an engineer.' (Farina's reaction, remembers Issigonis, was to roar with laughter!)[53] In Italy, though, the world *stile* does not have the pejorative connotations of American chrome cosmetics and the annual model change so abhorred by British industrial designers, for Italian stylists come from the coachbuilding profession and have always been capable of extremely creative body engineering.

In fact, Issigonis had great respect for the work of 'Pinin' and was well satisfied with the treatment of the 1100. He and Sergio ('Pinin's son) also became firm friends. (According to Alex Moulton, 'Pinin' delegated Sergio to do the 1100 styling.)

The decision to use Pininfarina for the external form was an outstanding success. The lines were 'sharp' and pleasing, and sales figures were to vindicate the use of the Italian consultant. Though the ugly duckling Mini was endearing as an economy car, it seems likely that similar visual idiosyncrasy would not have been a success in the bigger class, where buyers

THE AUSTIN ROVER GROUP (B.M.I.H.T.)

Another view of the mock-up for a 1.5 litre family car developed by Issigonis on his return from Alvis. It became the starting point for the Issigonis front-wheel drive cars.

expected a certain degree of elegance for their money. However, the 1100 also had the sterling virtues of Issigonis's Mini layout: maximum internal volume (a precious commodity in what was still quite a small car), a long wheelbase relative to its overall length, reducing the unpleasant 'pitch' effect over bumps, and outstanding roadholding and handling.

The 1100 also had the long-awaited 'Hydrolastic' suspension, with the rubber spring units interconnected front to rear by fluid, which had been developed by Alex Moulton and first tested by him and Issigonis on the experimental Alvis (see pp. 37–9).

At the time, the ride of the 1100 was widely considered to be a revelation in such a small car,

though it did display a certain harsh choppiness over very bumpy surfaces that was not to everyone's taste. Later, Moulton was to substitute gas reservoirs in the system as a spring to soften the 'bounce mode', and this Hydragas system continued in production on British Leyland cars until 1981. In retrospect Moulton considers the earliest Hydrolastic system 'a caricature', and the gas element a great improvement. 'I was always all for gas. We were just frightened of it; we didn't know if we could keep it in.'[54] Today, from Moulton's perspective, 'the 1100 was a much more significant car than the Mini, and the true 'Supermini' prototype' – the predecessor of the ubiquitous space-efficient cars of today like the Golf and the Uno.

THE AUSTIN ROVER GROUP (B.M.I.H.T.)

The original Pininfarina design for the 1100. The contrived front end treatment was, wisely, dropped.

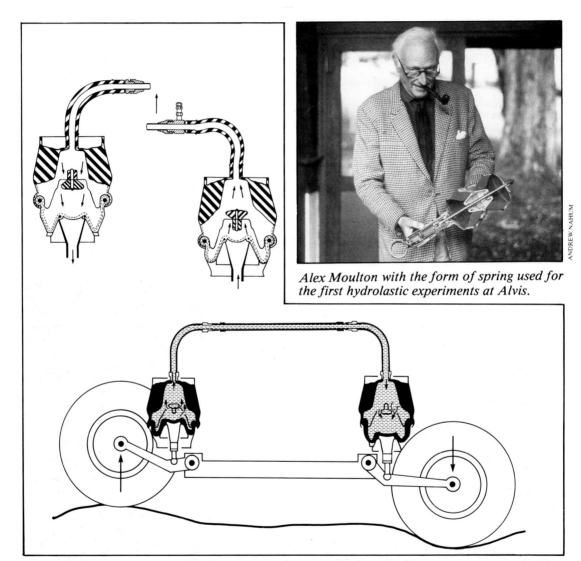

Alex Moulton with the form of spring used for the first hydrolastic experiments at Alvis.

ANDREW NAHUM

The hydrolastic system uses a fluid connection between the front and back springs on each side. The effect is to average out bumps and to give greater ride comfort. The first attempt at interconnection arose when Moulton and Issigonis realised that the particular form of rubber spring used could also displace fluid. This evolved into the specialised spring/displacer units for the 1100.

Launched in 1962 with a Morris badge (the Austin version followed the next year), the 1100 was immediately popular. In fact it was the most successful BMC car to date, making up one third of the company's British sales, and out-selling the Mini by a considerable margin. The fight was now on for the middle ground of the British car market, for Ford launched the Cortina in the same year. The two cars offered similar performance and accommodation, but whereas the 1100 offered Italian styling with Issigonis's new body 'package', a condensed engine/drive-line and front-wheel drive, the Cortina had a classical front engine/rear-wheel drive layout, and debased American styling. This is the simple mechanical formula, we are told, that the important fleet market desires. The legend of the Cortina and its success has grown so strong in recent years that it is a surprise to recall that for the first eight years of its life, until 1970, Issigonis's 1100 actually outsold the Ford product in Britain. The crunch came as Ford planners adeptly took the Cortina upmarket to cater to the growing prosperity and aspirations of their customers. In effect, they divided up the market into narrow strata, which they then targeted individually with a range of cars from basic economy models to high specification versions. There were trim and cosmetic changes, and larger engine options. By contrast, BMC soldiered on with the 1100, substantially unchanged, until, too late, it suddenly dawned on the management that their outstanding success had become old-fashioned.

COURTESY MRS GEORGE DOWSON

The Hotel de Paris, Monte Carlo. Left to right: Laurence Pomeroy, Alex Moulton, Mrs George Dowson, Dick Bursi (a designer at BMC), Alec Issigonis, Charles Griffin (with cigar), George Dowson. Taken c.1960, when the 1100 project was in full swing.

Above: *Pininfarina involvement was wisely continued with the 1800. This is thought to be the first study, in 1959, for the new car. The Torinese stylists kept the same unhappy front end treatment already seen on an 1100 mock-up.* Below: *This is believed to be the second Pininfarina study for the 1800 (1962).*

The Later Production Cars

Compared to continental manufacturers, British car makers in the decades after the Second World War were extraordinarily conservative, and deeply suspicious of design innovation. However, Issigonis had conceived and managed to 'sell' to his management the three most original mass-market cars built here in that period. Not only that, but they had proved extremely popular with the public. This success placed Issigonis in a position of immense prestige within BMC. He became technical director, with design responsibility for all the company's passenger cars, and gained a seat on the board. He was the biggest celebrity in the British motor industry, and probably the only industry figure who could urbanely address a wider audience. 'He was absolutely terrific with journalists' says Bill Boddy of *Motor Sport*, a long-standing doyen of motoring writers. 'He was very quick on the uptake', Ron Unsworth recalls, 'No other director could argue with him.'[55] There was no doubt that Issigonis's view of the evolution of the car was the one BMC was going to follow. But there were to be no more revolutions. The last Issigonis cars were to be scaled-up versions of the Mini/1100 theme, compromised in appearance by an enforced commonality of certain body parts, and Issigonis's cavalier attitude to car aesthetics.

The immediate priority, after the launch of the 1100, was to find a replacement for the ageing Farina-designed 1.5 litre car – badge-engineered simultaneously as the Morris Oxford, Austin Cambridge, Riley 1.5, Wolseley 16/60 and MG Magnette! Issigonis had proved the advantages of his transverse engine, front-wheel drive formula, and it must have seemed obvious that the 'stretched Mini' formula should be applied again. The car was to use the established 'B'-series 1600 cc engine, but during development the decision was taken to use the

1800 cc version, developed for the MGB sports car. It appears that the car itself also grew during development to take advantage of the extra available power. The result, which appeared in 1965 as the Austin 1800, was now rather too big for the market niche originally intended for it, while its unusual looks found few admirers. ('Land crab' became a general nickname.)

It cannot be denied that Issigonis's front-wheel drive formula and general design philosophy produced tremendously spacious cars, and in the small classes, this was of the utmost value. However, the habitability problem in a car approaching the 2 litre engine size is no longer really acute, and the Issigonis shape did not, in fact, scale up well to this size of car. Though 'cheeky' in a small car, the short bonnet on the 1800 seemed to offend against some innate preconception of a 'golden mean' in car architecture.

It would not be right to imply that Issigonis's flair had deserted him by this period. Though Director of Engineering, he was intimately concerned in the actual design of the 1800, and just as passionate about his new creation. But, as he says 'I designed cars without any prompting from my employers to suit what they wanted for sale. I thought I knew better than the market research people what the public wants – as is shown by the results.'[56] The problem is that backing one man's taste is a very high risk strategy for a large company – and no one can be right every time. Just one unsuccessful new model makes almost any car company reel – but in this period BMC produced three models which failed to engender much sales enthusiasm.

Apart from appearance, there were other problems with the 1800. The compact front-wheel drive package put a lot of weight over the front wheels, and the steering was judged by many to be unacceptably heavy. In *British*

Leyland – the Truth about the Cars, Jeff Daniels opined that the 1800

> 'seemed almost wilfully to magnify the ergonomic shortcomings of its smaller predecessors. Here once again was the ''bus driver'' steering-wheel angle and the minor control switches beyond reasonable reach. Here . . . was an umbrella-handle handbrake about as far away from the driver as it can ever have been in a production saloon car. . . . What had seemed amiable eccentricities in the Mini became annoyances in the bigger and more expensive car.'[57]

Nor was the build quality good enough to win the car friends in spite of its looks, as was the case with other 'ugly ducklings' from Saab and Volvo. Early unreliability gave it a bad reputation, and helped kill the car as a big earner for the company. There were gearbox problems and excessive oil consumption. This latter fault proved to be extremely elusive, until it was discovered that wrongly calibrated dipsticks caused the sump to be overfilled. Issigonis's design was not to be blamed for these niggling faults but, as Director of Engineering, build quality was ultimately his responsibility. His successes had all been won with tiny teams. On his own admission, and from the observations of his friends and colleagues, Issigonis never had the ambition to manage and drive a huge engineering department, but that, thanks to his achievements, was what he ended up having to do.

To fill the gap in the range between 1100 and 1800, BMC belatedly drew up the 'Maxi' project (launched in 1969), using a new 1500 cc engine that was under development. One curious constraint on the design of the car was that in order to save tooling costs the doors of the 1800 were to be used. These versatile doors, and the centre section pressings, had also been utilised in the

Austin 3 litre, unveiled in 1967! (This too was a 'typical' big Issigonis design, with very little charisma.) For the Maxi, the doors brought up the problem that the car could hardly be made much smaller than the 1800, or indeed, cheaper. The car received a poor initial reception, partly for its lacklustre appearance, but also for an imprecise cable-operated gearchange. However, in many respects it embodied the Issigonis ideals of practicality well: it had a hatchback, when few other saloons offered that facility, and with rear seat folded could carry a grandfather clock! It thus had generous internal room, and a high fifth gear for economical cruising – a comparative innovation at the time.

The Maxi was, though, the last production car from the Issigonis stable. The era of Donald Stokes and the Leyland take-over had arrived. From then on the cars were to be less individualistic, and, taking a leaf out of Ford's book, designs were intended to be more accurately targeted in order to satisfy consumer preferences.

Mini engineering writ large. The engine bay of the 1800.

Above: *An 1800 design modified at Longbridge from a Pininfarina original. No longer can Issigonis claim to 'design everything'.* Below: *The 1800, as finalised for production. For reasons of production expediency, the 1.5 litre car grew to share the 1800cc engine intended for the MGB sports car. The basic architecture of the car might well have worked in the 1.5 litre size, but even the flair of Pininfarina cannot conceal the lumpiness of the car.*

Above: *Initial thoughts for the intermediate family car that became the Maxi, and* (below) *as finalised for production. If the aim of BMC had specifically been to de-mythologise the passenger car they could scarcely have done better. Unfortunately, the customers had opinions too.*

THE AUSTIN ROVER GROUP (B.M.I.H.T.)

NATIONAL MOTOR MUSEUM

Austin 3-litre. Seldom can 'rationalisation' have extended so far as to make one set of doors do for three car models, running from 1.5 to 3 litres engine capacity. Launched in 1967, the 3-litre found few friends.

THE AUSTIN ROVER GROUP (B.M.I.H.T.)

THE AUSTIN ROVER GROUP (B.M.I.H.T.)

The 9X – Issigonis's replacement Mini – was axed by Donald Stokes soon after he took over. It was a more radical car than the Metro which eventually replaced the Mini.

Finale

One of the first casualties of the Stokes take-over in 1968 was Issigonis's pet project – the 9X Mini replacement. In an oft-quoted remark, Stokes claimed to have arrived at BMC to find 'the cupboard bare' of future models, except the 9X. This was a pioneering hatchback, in a quite advanced state of development, and Stokes seems to have been impressed with it. However, he regarded the new Mini as a low priority compared to a conventional car with which to attack the lucrative fleet market. It caused the team, and particularly Issigonis, bitter disappointment. 'The people who took us over thought they could do better. Well, I left it to them.'[58] Issigonis believes that this decision was the first nail in the coffin and, speaking in 1978, said that if it had been built, 'I personally feel we wouldn't have been in the trouble we're in now.' It is an attractive idea; the 9X had an all-new engine and was a much more radical car than the eventual replacement, the Metro, in which new bodywork clothes little altered Mini running-gear. The Golf and Renault 5 showed just how saleable the new generation of 'Superminis' was. Could the 9X have been in this class? Probably not. The appearance was rather boxy, and like the Mini, it was still tiny. The others were half a size bigger than the Mini – just a shade more roomy, without losing the convenience for urban use. It is also questionable whether the company had the technical resources and simple quality of build at the time to have fully exploited the 9X.

Issigonis was moved sideways when Stokes brought in Harry Webster from Triumph to be Chief Engineer and to direct the development of a new medium-sized model that, with breath-taking optimism, was known in the company as a 'Cortina Eater'. The result was the Marina. One motoring journal quipped that 'If you lived in Czechoslovakia, the Marina would seem like a good car.' Its dynamic behaviour on the road was grossly inferior to the Issigonis cars, the technical specification crude, and the appearance a banal pastiche of utterly conventional styling motifs. The greatest irony was that below the skin, much of this new, pragmatic car was actually based on running-gear, suspension and chassis parts from Issigonis's now venerable Morris Minor! However, the increased power and weight of the car (combined with a softening of the springing in the search for comfort) meant that it had no vestiges of the Minor's excellent handling and balance. And as is so often the way with such schemes, it transpired that considerable detailed redesign was needed, requiring new tooling and thus largely cancelling out the savings promised by recycling elements of the Minor design. In production terms though, the crash Marina programme was a heroic effort on the part of British Leyland designers and engineers, and it succeeded in fulfilling Stokes's objective by capturing fleet sales (outselling the Maxi by two to one), and earning desperately needed revenue.

Issigonis, however, had nothing to do with this project, nor with the inept re-bodying of the classic 1100 (latterly 1300) to produce the Allegro – a project described by one British Leyland watcher as the company's 'vital stumble'.[59]

For British Leyland the problem seems to have been in making the change from an 'inspirational' approach to the origination of new models, dependent on the insights of one highly talented individual, to committee-based product planning in line with modern motor industry precepts. Ford was the model of this approach, but that company had a long-established internal culture that made the process work. British Leyland was feeling its way into the age of a new type of management, but consequently falling between two stools. It was an uncomfortable transition. During this period, in Alex Moulton's view, the company fortunes went from 'merely losing money to disaster'.[60]

Issigonis has spoken little of his feelings during this period. Since the new policies were the antithesis of everything he had advocated, one could surmise that he must have hated the new régime of stop-gap engineering, expediency, and trashy styling. Moulton believes that Issigonis was completely out of sympathy with Webster and thereafter 'retired to a cell',[61] immersing himself in his own experimental projects, and keeping out of the day-to-day process of bringing on the new designs.

Recently Lord Stokes has explained his view of Issigonis and the design re-organisation he instituted at that time:

'A brilliant innovator who'd conceived a complete new breed of cars. . . . A very great man. A very charming man, one of the most charming men you could possibly meet. But he was also a very dominant engineer. . . . You can't have one man, as a maestro, running a huge engineering department. . . . It's got to be a team effort. He was the right man in his day, and I think events had almost overtaken him.'[62]

Alex Moulton's view of this period is just as illuminating, though from a quite different perspective:

'Alec was in the habit of being in total technical charge, answerable directly to the Managing Director, . . . and any other arrangement of working he would find impossible. He'd made his own personal choice. He didn't like the change of events which happened at the Leyland take-over

and he made his choice. *He had a wonderful run!*'[63]

Some colleagues believe that Issigonis was much happier when free to return to working alone on specific projects. He had never claimed any interest in the management of an engineering department, and now spent his time on a great variety of absorbing experiments. There was the steam Mini, with boiler and steam engine in a conventional Mini shell. Issigonis lost interest when he realised that fuel economy was just not competitive. Engine design also began to engage his attention: 'Until the last two or three years, I never really was an expert on engines; now I've become one of the great experts – but probably it will never be recognised.' In particular, he preached the virtues of the small in-line six-cylinder, reputedly designing one with a block merely 18 inches (0.44 m) long, and arguing 'We're looking for refinement, not power.'[64]

Following his retirement in 1971, he has continued to work actively as a consultant on a variety of advanced projects. The best-known is a 'gearless' Mini, in which a large engine drives through a torque converter, with one single drive ratio (said to be delightful to drive). The theory is that the higher cost and inefficiency of an oversized engine is countered by the weight and cost saved by discarding the gearbox. He also schemes improvements to the standard Mini which the company evaluates, and works on advanced engines and transmissions which derive from the 9X project.

The company also says that Issigonis is still consulted for his opinion on all new models, although he is not known to have had any significant input into any new production car since his retirement. His judgement is still highly respected, and he is asked to give future projects the benefit of his practical approach. He has access to the management of Austin Rover (now

Finale

First fruit of the new pragmatic Stokes era: the 'Cortina eater'. Issigonis had no hand in the design. Some elements of his original Morris Minor were recycled in the lack-lustre Marina.

Allegro: 'The vital stumble'. The development of the 1100 to produce the Allegro again proceeded without any input from Issigonis.

the Rover Group) at the highest levels, and is provided with a project engineer and two assistants to develop his projects. Rod Bull, the engineer, sees Issigonis daily and is adamant that these projects are not just a retirement hobby for him. 'There's always a possibility that things Sir Alec has designed will appear in cars on the road. It's very rewarding to work with Issigonis.'[65]

From our perspective, many years later, the BMC era reveals a great dilemma in industrial management. Individuals can make brilliant decisions. Perhaps committees can just make sound ones. If the product planning approach had been rigorously applied, the company would probably never have dared risk novel solutions like the Mini and 1100. But as it happened, the design brilliance of Issigonis was complemented by the flair and business acumen of Leonard Lord. But this kind of success is perhaps too dependent on the actual personalities involved and the coincidence of getting the right team. When BMC no longer had someone as tough and astute as Lord at the helm, the cars seemed just to miss the mark. Corporate hierarchies and decisions reached by formalised procedures give some insurance against the ebb and flow of talent in organisations.

Issigonis himself, somewhat curiously, appears to regard the large 1800 as his most successful car, but his incisive judgement may be less sound in this sector, and he has himself said 'I was really weaned on Austin Sevens, so it is perhaps natural that in my professional work I dislike designing big cars.'[66] It is also fair to point out that his role as technical director latterly deprived him of the chance to get really involved with individual car projects, and to apply his special analytical gifts to them. He did not want the accompanying administrative burden, and, as Jack Daniels says, 'All "Issi" wanted was to take one car and make it work.'[67]

The last word should perhaps rest with Ron Unsworth: 'None of them were committee motor cars; just one man breaking all the rules. It's not cheap to work that way, but he revolutionised the world's motoring.'[68]

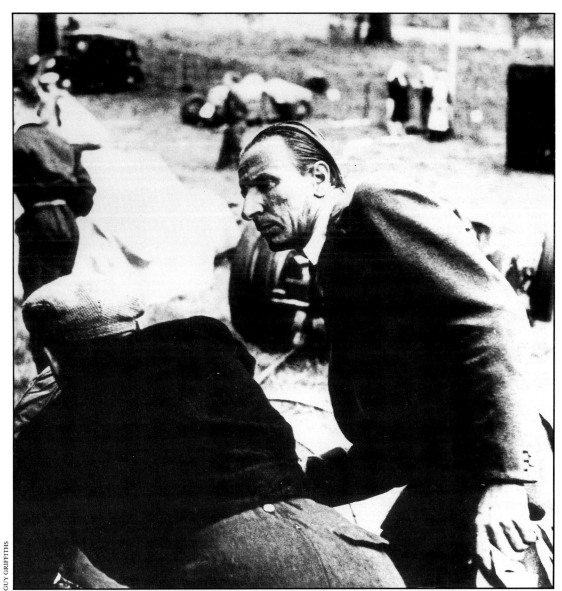

GUY GRIFFITHS

The look of intent concentration which struck his associates. 'He was very quick on the uptake. No other director could argue with him.' (Prescott hillclimb, September 1947.)

Volkswagen Golf

Fiat Uno

Postscript

Since the Mini, almost every European and Japanese manufacturer has developed a small car with a highly compact mechanical package, and the 'Supermini' has become a standard class. Though these cars without exception use front-wheel drive and a transversely mounted engine to keep the bonnet short, none can really be called an imitation of the Mini. It seems that the Mini's existence has spurred other designers to create an article of similar utility, using their own solutions. Transmission layouts are different to the Mini, and as yet, no other manufacturer has adopted rubber suspension or the later hydrolastic or hydragas variants, in spite of their excellent attributes.

Superminis have shown the capacity to be developed to astonishing standards of handling and performance, making purpose-designed sporting exotics seem irrelevant, as with the celebrated Golf GTI. In the Fiat Uno, a subtle adaption of the architecture of the Supermini, making it a little higher, has given a striking improvement in spaciousness. The imminent development of a stepless automatic gear for this class of car also promises further progress in utility. The ergonomic and engineering constraints of the mini-car may be severe, but its design evolution continues to progress.

NISSAN (UK) LTD

Nissan Micra

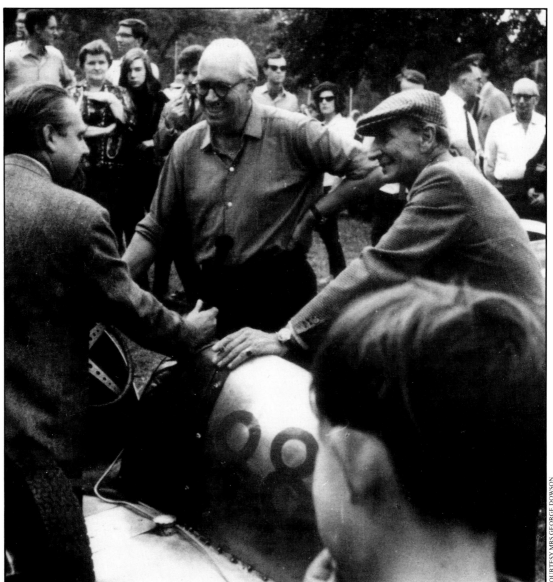

Alec Issigonis (right) with George Dowson (centre) being interviewed for a BBC programme. Prescott hillclimb, c. 1960.

Further Reading

(Full publication details, where not shown, appear in the Notes, pp 87–8.)

In general, car design is not so much written about as industrial design (although there is an extensive but often uncritical literature for motoring enthusiasts). Furthermore, the actual process of car design takes place as a secretive activity, well buried within the companies, who do not encourage their staff to 'put themselves about' with the media in a way that might, for example, be appropriate for an Italian designer of Expresso machines. Issigonis has always avoided expressing himself in print ('I find writing a disagreeable occupation') and, unlike many successful engineers and designers, never addressed professional bodies or learned societies: hence the literature is restricted. However, Issigonis has often spoken frankly in interviews, and much of the material in this monograph comes from the personal recollections of Issigonis and of others who participated in the creation of his cars.

For biography and for glimpses of the character of Issigonis, the following are useful: L J K Setright *The Designers*; and R Barker and A Harding (eds) *Automobile Design: Great Designers and their Work*. Laurence Pomeroy, friend of Issigonis and son of the famous Vauxhall designer, wrote *The Mini Story*, a good account of the development of the Mini, which also contains useful anecdotes and forms a pen picture of Issigonis. The detailed development of the cars is dealt with by Paul Skilleter in *Morris Minor*, and by Rob Golding in *Mini* (London, Osprey, 1979). The later cars are reviewed by Jeff Daniels in *British Leyland, the Truth about the Cars*.

There is some useful background material on the general development of the small car in Ian Ward *Motoring for the Millions* (Poole, Blandford Press, 1981). One professional who has written in detail about the process of car design is Dante Giacosa of Fiat in *Forty Years of Design with Fiat* (Milan, Automobilia, 1979), and his account does cover the development of miniature cars, although these were conceived on a different plan to the Mini. There have also been numerous historical articles in the enthusiast press, for example, on the Minor, by Jonathan Wood (*Thoroughbred and Classic Cars*, April 1981) and on the Mini, by Christie Campbell (ibid., September 1979).

For more technical comment on automotive engineering, see the *Proceedings of the Institution of Mechanical Engineers (Automobile Division)*: Transverse Engines – the First Decade, by E G Bareham (1969–70) *Proceedings* 184, 2A(4) pp 55–85. In the USA, the Society of Automotive Engineers Inc publishes useful papers.

Competing in the Lightweight Special.

Notes

1   R Barker and A Harding (eds) (1970) *Automobile Design: Great Designers and their Work*. Newton Abbot, David & Charles, p 319.
2   L J K Setright (1976) *The Designers*. Chicago, Follett, p 31.
3   A A C Issigonis in 'The Ironmonger', BBC Radio 4, 18 November 1986.
4   Ibid.
5   J Bolster (1949) *Specials*. London, Foulis & Co, pp 113–21.
6   Mrs George Dowson in conversation with the author 1986.
7   R Barker and A Harding, *op cit*. p 300.
8   P Skilleter (1981) *Morris Minor*. London, Osprey, p 18.
9   A E Moulton in conversation with the author 1986.
10 J Daniels in conversation with the author 1985.
11 A A C Issigonis, writing in the Introduction to L Pomeroy (1964) *The Mini Story*. London, Temple Press.
12 M Thomas (1964) *Out on a Wing*. London, Michael Joseph, p 221.
13 Ibid p 222.
14 P Skilleter, *op cit*. pp 17–18.
15 J Daniels in conversation with the author 1985.
16 Ibid.
17 A E Moulton in 'The Ironmonger' *op cit*.
18 M Thomas *op cit*. p 236.
19 P Skilleter *op cit*. p 22.
20 Ibid p 33.
21 R Barker and A Harding, *op cit*. p 303.
22 A A C Issigonis, *op cit*.
23 P Skilleter *op cit*. p 58.
24 R Barker and A Harding, *op cit*. p 320.
25 A A C Issigonis, in L Pomeroy *op cit*.
26 A E Moulton (1979) Innovation. *Journal of the Royal Society of Arts*, 128: pp 31–44.
27 S Bayley in *Car* December 1982, p 68.
28 M Thomas *op cit*. p 181.
29 A E Moulton in conversation with the author 1986.
30 A E Moulton and A Best (1979) From Hydrolastic to Hydrogas Suspension, *Proceedings of the Institution of Mechanical Engineers* 193 (9) pp 15–37.
31 A E Moulton (1979) *op cit*.
32 R Barker and A Harding *op cit*. p 310.
33 A E Moulton in conversation with the author 1986.
34 R Barker and A Harding *op cit*. p 310.
35 J Daniels in conversation with the author 1985.
36 R Barker and A Harding *op cit*. p 310.
37 A E Moulton in conversation with the author 1986.
38 L Pomeroy *op cit*. p 37.
39 R Unsworth, in conversation with the author 1985.
40 Ibid.
41 J Daniels in conversation with the author 1985.
42 R Unsworth in conversation with the author 1985.
43 J Sheppard in 'The Ironmonger' *op cit*.
44 J Daniels in conversation with the author 1985.
45 Ibid.
46 A A C Issigonis, quoted by R Unsworth, in conversation with the author 1985.
47 J Daniels in conversation with the author 1985.
48 Ibid.
49 L Pomeroy *op cit*. p 51.
50 J Daniels in conversation with the author 1985.
52 R Unsworth in conversation with the author 1985.
53 L Pomeroy *op cit*. p 69.

53   A A C Issigonis in 'The Ironmonger' *op cit*.
54   A E Moulton in conversation with the author 1986.
55   R Unsworth in conversation with the author 1985.
56   A A C Issigonis in 'The Ironmonger' *op cit*.
57   J Daniels (1980) *British Leyland, the Truth about the Cars*. London, Osprey, p 73.
58   A A C Issigonis in 'The Ironmonger' *op cit*.
59   J Daniels (1980) *op cit*.
60   A E Moulton in 'The Ironmonger' *op cit*.
61   Ibid.
62   Lord Stokes in 'The Ironmonger' *op cit*.
63   A E Moulton in 'The Ironmonger' *op cit*.
64   R Barker and A Harding, *op cit*. p 318.
65   R Bull in conversation with the author 1986.
66   A A C Issigonis in L Pomeroy *op cit*.
67   J Daniels (1980) *op cit*.
68   R Unsworth in conversation with the author 1985.

MODERN EUROPEAN DESIGNERS
A biographical record of 20th century designers

Other titles in this series:

	Price
MISHA BLACK By Avril Blake	£7.50
MILNER GRAY By Avril Blake	£8.50
HARRY PEACH Dryad and the DIA By Pat Kirkham	£9.50
ERNEST RACE By Hazel Conway	£6.50
DOUGLAS SCOTT By Jonathan Glancey	£8.95
ETTORE SOTTSASS JNR By Penny Sparke	£6.50
MARIANNE STRAUB By Mary Schoeser	£8.95

Copies are available from all good bookshops,
or by post (add £1.50 post and packing per title)
from
Design Centre Bookshop,
28 Haymarket, London SW1Y 4SU.